NEXT

To The Culbreaths,
My family in
Christ! May God
continue to bless
you abundantly!

[signature]

NEXT

Surviving a
Leadership Transition

MARVIN ANTHONY MOSS

Abingdon Press
Nashville

NEXT
SURVIVING A LEADERSHIP TRANSITION

Library of Congress Cataloging-in-Publication Data

Moss, Marvin Anthony.
  Next : surviving a leadership transition / by Marvin Anthony Moss ; with a foreword by US Ambassador Andrew Young.
    pages cm
  ISBN 978-1-4267-5102-8 (alk. paper)
1. Christian leadership. 2. Church management. 3. Occupational mobility.
4. Moss, Marvin Anthony—Ethics. I. Title.
  BV652.1.M67 2013
  253—dc23
                                                                2013031911

13 14 15 16 17 18 19 20 21 22—10 9 8 7 6 5 4 3 2 1
MANUFACTURED IN THE UNITED STATES OF AMERICA

This book is dedicated to my mom, Bernice Moss, who is still with me, and to my dad, SSGT. Marvin Moss, USA Ret., who went home to be with the Lord in 1986. Their sacrifices and belief in me empowered me to keep fighting the good fight of faith. To my mom for making me read National Geographic *so that I travel without leaving the house and to my dad, who served in the United States Army and made it possible for us to actually visit some of the places that we read about. I love them for exposing me to different cultures and truly helping me understand how to love all of God's people regardless of race, creed, or color.*

CONTENTS

Contents

FOREWORD

Marvin Moss has written a pastoral epistle about transition. In reality it is about life in the Christian congregation.

As a young pastor in my first two country churches in Thomasville and Beachton, Georgia, in 1955, I could have used some of this voice of faith and experience. But since there was no such guidance at hand, I made many of the mistakes that this book could have helped me avoid. A wise and tolerant group of "salt of the earth" Christians nurtured me for three short, wonderful years and then sent me forth into the world both chastened and humbled.

Those years in rural Georgia with a congregation filled with brilliant minds but also life's trials and tribulations taught me that the true faith of the church comes via the Holy Spirit in the life of the people—their daily dependence on God's amazing grace and boundless mercy.

Doctor Moss has lived through and grown in congregations filled with the faith and love of similar pastorates, but the variety of his experience has forced him to become more analytical in his chronicles of Christian experience. However, I don't see this as just a book for pastors about church transitions.

As I have moved through ministries with the National Council of Churches, the Civil Rights Movement, Congress, the United Nations, Atlanta City Hall, The Olympic Games, and numerous corporate responsibilities, I find the message resonating throughout life's callings.

Business is a ministry; teaching is a ministry; medicine is a ministry; and so is every life well lived. Marvin Moss has given us guideposts that are relevant to every aspect of Christian faith and citizenship.

In these turbulent times it is important that we ground ourselves in the experience of faith, service, leadership, and servanthood that Dr. Moss shares with us in this narrative of service and devotion.

—Andrew Young
Former UN Ambassador

ACKNOWLEDGMENTS

God's goodness and mercy have indeed followed me all the days of my life. As I was completing this project, which is my first, I began to think of all of the people whom God had allowed to cross my path. They have been with me from the time that I accepted my call into the ministry in August of 1993 to beginning my eighth year in my second appointment as the Senior Pastor of Cascade United Methodist Church in June 2013. The unfortunate thing is that I will not be able to mention all of the people who have enabled me to serve God and God's people in the way that I have. What a blessing!

When I accepted my call into the ministry, I was a member of Wesley Chapel UMC in Decatur, Georgia, and Rev. Leon Hollinshed was the pastor. I vividly remember approaching him with excitement, exclaiming that I felt God was calling me into the ministry. His reply was nowhere near what I had expected. He told me that if it indeed was God, then the same passion that I had at that moment would be the same passion I would have in approximately a year's time. To put it more plainly, he told me to take one more year to make sure! I am so grateful for his wisdom because after the year passed and I was able to move forward, I had an even greater appreciation for the journey I was about to embark upon. He told me that no matter how good it is or how bad it gets, always stick to preaching the word of God. *Thank you, sir, so much.*

My next pastor was Dr. Nick Harvey. He was appointed to Wesley Chapel UMC in June of 1994. As I served under him while I attended seminary and went through the ordination process, I truly experienced unconditional love and true mentoring. He created an associate pastor position for me and gave me an opportunity to serve and learn. He and his wife, Dr. Kyra Harvey, nurtured me, prayed for and with me, corrected me when necessary, and above all else, modeled for me true friendship. To this day, we are friends, and they cover me in prayer. *Thank you, Pastor and Kyra, for all that you have done and are doing and for all that you mean to me. I love you.*

This journey would not have been at all possible without Mr. Roger Young of Young's Funeral Home. Mr. Young was good friends with the late Bishop Cornelius Henderson, who was serving as president and dean of Gammon Theological Seminary. I worked for Mr. Young by driving limousines, and he said to me, "I see you as a preacher. Go to Gammon, and tell Reverend Henderson that I sent you and to let you in school." You see, I wanted to go to seminary but had no money and nowhere to get any money. I did as he told me, and the rest is history. The fact that Mr. Young was willing to use his name and relationship to take a chance on me was proof indeed God had something for me to do. *Brother Young, thank you for seeing in me what I didn't see in myself, and thank you for the mentoring and for the job driving for you.*

I want to sincerely thank Jennifer "JT" Thomas, president and founder of MediaReady Consulting. Thank you for pushing me, pestering me (smile), and putting up with me. Thank you for not letting me quit and put this project off, possibly never getting it done. You have had to endure a lot with just being as committed to this project as you were. You are the consummate professional and truly representative of the best that God has to offer. Thank you for your passion and dedication to this project and for always going the extra mile. You are a true friend, and I have been blessed by knowing you. You are most definitely a blessing to the Kingdom. *My sister, I love you and praise God for you!*

The late Bishop Cornelius Henderson allowed me to enter seminary with no money and on a promise to pay him back. He took a chance on me. As I would go to revivals with him and watch him interact with people and mentor and nurture future preachers, I felt inspired to serve God with excellence. He transcended racial barriers, denominational barriers, socioeconomic barriers, and any other threat to empowering God's people. Even though he passed on to his eternal reward before I had an opportunity to invite him to preach at my first appointment, I was blessed that when I arrived at my second appointment, his wife, Mrs. Dorothye C. Henderson, was a member there. She took up the mantle and picked up where Bishop Henderson left off. *Thank you, "Ma," for your love, your compassion, and your passion for helping young preachers succeed. Well, I was young when I started! I love you and count it a blessing to be able to call on you at any time.*

To all of the prayer warriors who have covered me with prayer both day and night and have supported me silently in person but cried out to the Lord asking for him to fight the battles, guide me through the valleys, and keep me in perfect peace—I love you!

To all of the wonderful people in the congregations that I have served—thank you for nurturing me, encouraging me, and above all, praying for me!

Last but not least, I want to thank my mom for all of the love and support that she has given me. It was her leadership as a military spouse that I observed and have been able to draw from as I have navigated through life thus far. She exhibited strength, courage, compassion, vision, and faith in God. She has truly inspired me to fight the good fight of faith and to know that God has plans for me. *I love you, Mom.*

INTRODUCTION

God has blessed me to be in position to receive some incredible assignments. As I am in my eighth year of my second appointment, it's amazing how God has proven over and over again that he is in control. There have been so many instances when I thought I had the plan, the vision, the formula, the education, and all of the other human attributes that a leader needs only to find out that God's plan is the one that prevails all of the time.

Suffice it to say, this book is about how I had to learn, sometimes the hard way, that if I do the basics—pray, fast, study, meditate, and love the people—then God could and would use what I brought to the table to do what he intended to do all along. Just like the little boy with two fish and five loaves of bread or the widow who gave all that she had, if we, both pastors and members, give it all that we have, then God can and will do a whole lot to meet the needs of the people we have been called to serve.

Next uses lessons that I learned as a child to demonstrate how conventional wisdom coupled with a little education and continual prayer can produce a fruitful experience. For example, one of the chapters in this book is entitled, "Are We There Yet?" In this chapter I share what would happen when my family took trips. My brother and I would get on my mother's last nerve by continually asking the proverbial question, *Are we there yet?* The essence of this chapter is to help individuals deal with impatience, disappointment, roadblocks, and detours that may appear to hinder them in getting the objective accomplished. However, we learn that all things work together for the good of those who love the Lord and are called according to his purpose.

As I mentioned earlier, God is in control. This book is intended to give leaders practical solutions to both common and unique situations and to share some personal experiences. Hopefully it will also give you a chuckle every now and then at some of the situations I found myself in and some of the things I did that maybe I shouldn't have done. It is also intended to move you to deep reflection, push you to prayer, and encourage you to keep on keeping on.

My prayer is that this book will position readers to enjoy the journey that God has them on and know at the end of the day that God is saying, "Well done, well done my good and faithful servant, well done!"

More of God, less of me. All of God, none of me!

CHAPTER ONE

Hi, My Name Is

Who We Are as Children of God and as
Spiritual Beings; Less about Accolades
and Accomplishments

"Good evening! This is your new pastor, and his name is Reverend Marvin Moss."

These were the words spoken by my district superintendent as he introduced me to the members of the Staff/Pastor-Parish Relations Committee of my first appointment on June 16, 1999. This nine-member committee represents the human resources arm of The United Methodist Church at the local level. I was thirty-six years old and excited to be assuming the position of senior pastor.

The introduction is an extremely significant part of a leadership transition. The only thing more important than the introduction itself is the person who is conducting it. The existing community is more apt to receive the idea of new leadership favorably if the person who is doing the introduction holds some position of accepted authority within the group. I say "accepted" because this means the person has developed enough social capital and earned the respect of the members on such a level that they trust his or her decision to introduce someone new. If the person who is introducing the new leader does not have a good rapport with the existing community, then this immediately positions the new leader in a negative light, despite the new leader possibly having a good track record of accolades and accomplishments. The person who is doing the introduction also needs to be someone who can represent the new leader well. How often have we witnessed the immediate dismissal of campaign managers and other high-level participants of a political party when they have done or said something that did not positively reflect the character of the individual who was running for a particular office?

All too often a new leader may believe that personal accolades and accomplishments, résumés, and report cards will ensure a smooth transition. Far from it. The introduction initiates the process for the new leader to demonstrate a level of emotional attachment when going into a new community. It is through this emotional attachment that possibilities will be opened for the existing members to feel, rather than read about, who the new leader is.

A NEW LEADER MAY BELIEVE THAT PERSONAL ACCOLADES AND ACCOMPLISHMENTS, RÉSUMÉS, AND REPORT CARDS WILL ENSURE A SMOOTH TRANSITION. FAR FROM IT.

After the district superintendent's introduction, I quickly realized that just because he had introduced me as the new pastor and put the title *reverend* in front of my name, I was not automatically home free. I had some work to do on my personal introduction before the congregation embraced me as its trusted new leader. This congregation had a strong sense of family, and the members had prepared themselves to endure yet another leadership change. They all seemed to have the same question about me: "Who is this inexperienced unknown who's trying to become a part of our family?"

While it sounds a bit harsh, their wariness was actually quite normal. Every congregation goes through a range of emotions when there is a leadership change. Depending upon the level of the relationship between the membership and the previous leader, the incoming leader must first be prepared to focus more on getting a good read of the membership than on establishing a position of control and authority. Getting a good read refers to accurately assessing the different factors that come together to make up the existing membership or community. While a myriad of dynamics exist, some of the more weighty ones may include personality types, median age of the group, communal values, and level of emotional attachment to certain historical aspects of the church's existence. Many memberships are unable to embrace any type of change because of an entrenchment in the way things have always been done.

THE INCOMING LEADER MUST FIRST BE PREPARED TO FOCUS MORE ON GETTING A GOOD READ OF THE MEMBERSHIP THAN ON ESTABLISHING A POSITION OF CONTROL AND AUTHORITY.

At my initial meeting with the aforementioned Staff/Pastor-Parish Relations Committee, I was greeted with blank stares. This meeting was conducted by a subset of individuals who spoke for the larger congregation. I knew the members had my bio and the district superintendent had given me a good introduction, but they didn't *know* me on a professional, personal, or pastoral level. I told them that, as part of our getting to know each other, I wanted to hear from each of them. I went around the room and listened to what they had to say. Doing this allowed me to hear what was important to them individually and let them know I was a person who would stop to listen to them. That initial meeting afforded me the opportunity to break the ice, calm the members' concerns, and begin to build a relationship. They were not really concerned with who I was; they were more concerned with what I was going to change and what they would have to give up.

Who Am I? Why Am I Here?

Beginning a new assignment is a daunting experience. Try stepping into the footsteps of a longtime leader, and you can easily be overcome with doubt. To truly be able to walk faithfully into the new position, you must remind yourself that God has called you into this leadership. You must let those you will lead know from the beginning that you are committed to creating a positive atmosphere and that you are also a listener. During the 1992 presidential campaign, Admiral James Stockdale, the running mate of candidate Ross Perot, appeared in the televised vice-presidential debate. He shocked the audience and later became the focus of comedic commentary and historical political humor when he began his opening remarks with the questions: "Who am I? Why am I here?" For many transitional leaders, this question, while initially amusing, is one that needs to be examined.

Who am I, and why am I here? Not only is it important for the congregation to know who you are, but it must also understand clearly why you are there. The *who* and *why* must parallel each other to the degree that the authenticity of your person is exhibited through your motive. For instance, the person who is motivated simply by position, power, prestige, or money will not exhibit the level of compassion, integrity, and genuine concern that needs to be in evidence to create a cohesive community. When the disciples were called into action, they had to leave their main source of income: "They immediately left their nets and followed Him." (Mark 1:18 NKJV). This particular passage of scripture helps us understand that leadership should emanate from a sincere desire to serve humanity rather than solely from the pursuit of dollars and cents.

In Exodus 3:11 Moses asks God the question, "Who am I, that I should go to Pharaoh, and bring the Israelites out of Egypt?" In Exodus 3:13 Moses asks another question: "Suppose I go to the Israelites and say to them, 'The God of your fathers has sent me to you,' and they ask me, 'What is his name?' Then what shall I tell them?" God responds to Moses in the next verse, "I AM WHO I AM. This is what you are to say to the Israelites: 'I AM has sent me to you.'" This scripture passage helps us understand that, with regard to transitional leadership, who we are as people of God is more important than who we are because of accolades and accomplishments. The understanding of whose we are as part of the kingdom of God and as children of God serves to keep us in a place of humility when, as the apostle Paul puts it, we begin to think better of ourselves than we should (Rom. 12:3).

While a level of pride is associated with each individual's personhood, it must be healthy pride in that we are always striving for excellence versus perfection. Excellence always pushes us to do the very best that we can but not at any cost. Perfection, on the other hand, causes us to be more concerned with our name as an individual than with a good name for the community.

I can remember as a child growing up, every time I would leave the house my mother would say to me, "Remember you are a Moss." My father was in the Army, which meant that at each new duty station we lived on post. This meant that if anyone in the Moss family acted in a manner that violated any of the rules or regulations of the community, my father would be the one held responsible for our actions. This meant that the commanding officer would send for him and not necessarily for the one in the family who had committed the infraction. If we did not keep the grass cut, the yard maintained, the trash cleaned up from the yard, and our quarters, or home, in good condition, we would be subject to expulsion from the community. Therefore, the Moss name carried weight.

Becoming the Servant Leader

When addressing a community as a new leader, it is imperative that the members receive you as a person whom God has named, or appointed, as the leader. Such a reception means that the existing community feels your passion and compassion for them and for their values. In some instances, this aspect of the transition is greatly enhanced when the outgoing leader participates in and supports the transition by handing off the baton, or affirming the incoming leader, in front of the community. This is a welcomed gesture, especially if the outgoing leader has had a long tenure with the existing membership and there is a great deal of respect and admiration for that person. One of the key learning points of the naming component of the transition process is that one's accolades and accomplishments are not as significant as one's ability to demonstrate a genuine sense of care and concern for the existing community. Whatever is done must be done in an authentic manner. The new leader must ooze sincerity. Some of the things that leader can do to express concern may include, but not be limited to, hospital visitations, letters of condolence sent to bereaved families if he or she is unable to attend a service, and phone calls to follow up with a family several weeks after a hospitalization or funeral service. I have been extremely blessed when I have taken ten or fifteen minutes out of a hectic day to make a hospital visitation to meet with a family who does not know whether or not their loved one will recover.

THE EXISTING COMMUNITY SHOULD FEEL YOUR PASSION AND COMPASSION FOR THEM AND FOR THEIR VALUES.

One such visit yielded a much different result than I had anticipated. Each day the front office sends a hospitalization census to all of the pastors so that we can keep up with the status of our sick and shut-in members. My administrative assistant had already planned my day to begin with a breakfast meeting, followed by several other meetings on the very same day. Even though I have clergy staff assigned to make routine visitations, I felt God tugging at me to cut my breakfast meeting short and make a visitation to pray with a family whose loved one was not doing well. As I entered the room, I was prepared to "be in charge" and "be the pastor." What happened actually blessed me for the rest of my day. Contrary to what I had expected to find, family members were already gathered around the bed, praying and singing hymns. When I walked in, the wife of the member who was ill exclaimed, "Pastor! We're glad you could come by. We didn't expect you because we know how busy you are." It was at that moment that I felt a piercing in my heart. You see, because while they knew my name, Marvin Anthony Moss, and they knew my position, senior pastor, I had not done a good job of helping them know my *heart*. They did not know that my greatest joy comes from being with God's people and walking with them through challenging times and celebrating with them during times of joy. The fact that this family thought my busy schedule was more important than being with them taught me a very valuable lesson. The people must know *whose* you are before they know *who* you are.

Situations like this hospital scenario serve to keep a person grounded and truly focused on the foundational element of being a great leader. That is, expressing genuine concern for the people you are leading and sincere passion for serving them. It is through this servant leadership model that people will begin to know not only who you are but also whose you are. Careful attention, however, must be given to the fact that not everyone will be able to receive this kind of personalized attention. Depending upon the number of individuals for whom you have responsibility, you may need to be creative with adding that personal touch. This means handwritten notes may not necessarily be written by *your* hand, but their message should still be given by you, and you should be diligent in trying to sign them all. Again, the intent is to express sincere care and concern, which in turn will allow the people in your church to embrace your heart.

Less about Accolades and Accomplishments

Some people feel more comfortable when they know that their leader has some level of demonstrated ability. In this instance, accomplishments, accolades, and academic achievement do play a role in establishing a platform from which you can operate. But others are put off by leaders who make much of their past successes. Therefore, a delicate balance must be established in which individuals are aware of your status but not intimidated by it. With the passage of time, they will become even more aware of your intellectual skill set.

While the natural inclination is to position yourself to intentionally advertise who you are, I would caution against leading with this technique. It has been my experience that in this highly technological age, before you have even reached your assignment, someone has already Googled you and is keenly aware of what you are bringing to the table. Therefore, I would strongly suggest you lead with your heart first, in case they have Googled the wrong person, someone who happens to have the same name as you. On a more serious note, just be comfortable with not giving in to pressure to prove who you are and instead *show* them who you are. As The Consolers sing, "May the work I've done speak for me."

You should place more focus on operating in such a manner that the respect and admiration you receive are earned rather than demanded. I had one of my mentors tell me that if you have to tell the people you are the pastor, then you are not the pastor. Similarly, one of my seminary professors, the late Bishop L. Scott Allen, reminded our entire class that, while the bishop may appoint you to a church to serve as its pastor, it is the people who *make* you the pastor. This statement exemplifies the point I referenced earlier regarding leading with your heart and not your accomplishments. As I started settling down in my first appointment, I realized that people clearly understood that the bishop had appointed me, that I had graduated from Gammon Theological Seminary with a Master of Divinity degree, that I had graduated from Hampton University with a Bachelor of Science degree in business management, and that I had graduated from the Navy Reserve Chaplain Officers Training School. While the congregation was aware of my accolades and accomplishments, the expectation was that I would roll up my sleeves and get my hands dirty, just as the members did when it came to taking care of God's house called St. James United Methodist Church.

THE RESPECT AND ADMIRATION YOU RECEIVE SHOULD BE EARNED RATHER THAN DEMANDED.

When I arrived at St. James, I found the members joined together as a family to take care of the needs of the church. For example, facility maintenance, which included janitorial duties, administrative duties, and landscaping, were all taken care of by a few of the members. These were the members who had been at the church for quite some time and were descendants of the people who had built the church. Basically, when the going got rough, they were the tough ones who stuck it out to ensure the church survived. So to them, accomplishments and accolades were not important. The important questions they had for me were, "Do you love my Jesus?" and "Do you love my church?" Having fully embraced the culture that existed there and sincerely desiring to be a part of the family, I took the initiative to get things done. The day after my first Sunday preaching, I went to the church early in the morning to help with cleaning up from the day before. I was the first to arrive and took advantage of the opportunity to start working. This demonstrated that I desired to be a part of their level of commitment to the church and to the people whom I had been called to serve. I chose cleaning the restrooms as my first task. As I was wrapping up, a couple of the members who came regularly to clean showed up and expressed their surprise at seeing me there, moreover at seeing me cleaning the restrooms. One of them exclaimed, "Pastor, you do toilets?" To which I replied with a smile, "It's easier now than it was when I was a child. At least now I don't have to use a toothbrush to do it." That gave us all a good laugh. I then told them how blessed I felt to be a part of the family.

After I had put away the cleaning materials and taken out the garbage, I returned to my office and began checking my voice mail messages. Somewhere around the third message, I thought, "What a nice gesture it would be to go and buy lunch for those members who are here cleaning." But when I asked what I could get them, they replied, "Oh, no, we're going home for lunch. Would you like to come with us?" My initial reaction was to run down a mental list of all the things I had to get done that would prevent me from going. Then I realized that it would be a better use of my time to go and eat lunch and fellowship with them in an informal setting. I must admit that while at lunch, I had to struggle to let down my guard so I would be in a more relaxed state of mind and better able to get to know who they were and not worry about what they might be up to.

This suspicion on my part is not an uncommon feeling to have. The unfortunate reality is that many new leaders are skeptical and on the defensive when it comes to being invited into an intimate setting of existing members of the community. This state of mind is exacerbated if previous experiences have caused the new leader a great deal of distress. For instance, opportunities always present themselves for the new leader to be triangulated into situations and circumstances that existed long before he or she arrived on the scene. That is to say, if there is a group that has upheld a particular cause, then it will take the opportunity to pull the new leader onto its side by not fully disclosing its cause and presenting that cause as if the whole community supports it. I can remember the wise words of one of my mentors, Mr. William Lamar, a former chief marketing officer for McDonald's USA, who said to me, "Always be patient in your deliberation. Take the time to find out the opposing side of an issue someone is advocating." By recounting his wise advice during that lunch with the group of church cleaners, I was able to be present in the moment without positioning myself to take sides or prematurely embrace a particular direction or vision. By operating in this manner, I had the opportunity to present myself as a fair and genuine individual who was concerned about the welfare of the entire community and not a particular group.

BE PATIENT IN YOUR DELIBERATION. TAKE THE TIME TO FIND OUT THE OPPOSING SIDE OF AN ISSUE SOMEONE IS ADVOCATING.

The beauty of this entire situation was that it allowed me to learn more about myself apart from my accolades and accomplishments. For instance, was I really a person who possessed the ability to fairly and accurately assess both sides of an equation so as to operate as King Solomon did when deciding to whom the infant child belonged (1 Kgs. 3:16-28)? I recognized that it was imperative that, as a judge, I be fair and impartial, exhibiting the sometimes rare trait of authentic concern for the truth to be revealed. Inherently, we all like to think the best of ourselves. But the apostle Paul admonishes us in Romans 12:3: "I say to every one of you: Do not think of yourself more highly than you ought." We must be, and remain, humbled in our thinking so that we can be in a position for God, and not people, to elevate us.

CHAPTER TWO
FROM MOSES TO JOSHUA

Out with the Old, In with the New: Making Your
Transition Relational, Not Generational

"After the death of Moses the servant of the LORD, it came to pass that the LORD spoke to Joshua the son of Nun, Moses' assistant, saying: 'Moses My servant is dead. Now therefore, arise, go over this Jordan, you and all this people, to the land which I am giving to them—the children of Israel'" (Josh. 1:1-2 NKJV). Many have used this passage to speak to change of leadership from a generational perspective rather than a relational one. All too often when this passage is used to deliver a message of theological significance, it is used to highlight "out with the old and in with the new!" During a leadership transition, a congregation's anxiety level is heightened because there is an expectation that change is going to take place. Any change represents a threat to the existing power brokers, as well as to those who have been in place for a long period of time and feel a sense of security. The incoming leader must be able to embrace the existing community and manage the change in such a manner that it is received in a less threatening way. I say "in a less threatening way" because it is a given that any change in any environment will initially be perceived as a threat.

ANY CHANGE IN ANY ENVIRONMENT WILL INITIALLY BE PERCEIVED AS A THREAT.

The scriptural reference cited earlier highlights a leadership transition that was taking place because of a death. The text states that after the death of Moses, Joshua was called to succeed him. Death necessitated a leadership change. However, I would like to focus on what happened prior to Moses' death that positioned Joshua to be able to transition into a place of leadership. "Now Joshua the son of Nun was full of the spirit of wisdom, for Moses had laid his hands on him; so the children of Israel heeded him, and did as the LORD had commanded Moses" (Deut. 34:9 NKJV). Before he died, Moses publicly affirmed Joshua as a leader—and not only as a leader but also as a leader capable of leading the people, from the youngest to the oldest. In addition to giving the people the assurance that Joshua was the right person to lead them, Moses also reassured Joshua in front of the people by telling him to be strong and of good courage, for Joshua would have to lead the people the rest of the way.

> Then Moses called Joshua and said to him in the sight of all Israel, "Be strong and of good courage, for you must go with this people to the land which the LORD has sworn to their fathers to give them, and you shall cause them to inherit it. And the LORD, He *is* the One who goes before you. He will be with you, He will not leave you nor forsake you; do not fear nor be dismayed. (Deut. 31:7-8 NKJV)

In addition to Joshua's demonstrated ability as a warrior, he received a more valuable form of affirmation: the seal of approval from his predecessor. Oftentimes the predecessor has been in place for an extended period of time and has formed important relationships with a great number of people in the community. If the outgoing leader is highly respected and loved, then his or her approval of the incoming leader means more than the résumé, gifts, and abilities of the incoming leader.

It is in this regard that we are able to understand that the leadership transition must include a public affirmation of the incoming leader in order for the transition to have a chance at being successful. Additionally, this public display also affirms that the new leader has the capacity to embrace all generations and aspects of the existing members. All too often the younger the leader, the more threatened the older community becomes. Conversely, the older the leader, the more threatened the younger members feel.

THE LEADERSHIP TRANSITION MUST INCLUDE A PUBLIC AFFIRMATION OF THE INCOMING LEADER IN ORDER FOR THE TRANSITION TO HAVE A CHANCE AT BEING SUCCESSFUL. THIS PUBLIC DISPLAY SHOULD AFFIRM THAT THE NEW LEADER HAS THE CAPACITY TO EMBRACE ALL GENERATIONS AND ASPECTS OF THE EXISTING MEMBERS.

Out with the Old, In with the New

Such was the case with my first appointment. The older members felt as though my youthful age would cause me to not be as concerned about them and value their input. However, the contrary was true. Because there was no public ceremony of affirmation by my predecessor but simply an introduction from a representative of the United Methodist conference, I realized that the transition would have to be relational and not generational. I will admit that at times

I felt as if I was on the television show *Survivor*, minus the cameras and the outtakes. If I were to survive this transitional period, I would have to relate to all members and be delicate in my time management. It would be imperative to embrace the entire membership from a perspective of desiring to become a part of the community and not trying to take it over. I also noticed that the younger members, who were louder, began expressing their excitement about my arrival. As a result, I had to spend twice as much time with the older members, assuring them that we would still operate as a family. This meant exhibiting to them that God had affirmed me and that the way I managed the concerns of the congregation served as an indication that I was capable of embracing this leadership change from a relational perspective and not a generational one.

My *Survivor*-like experience is not exclusive to The United Methodist Church but applies to pastors of all denominations. Bishop Joseph Walker III was only twenty-four and had just 175 members when he began his pastorate at Mount Zion Baptist Church in Nashville, Tennessee, which today has more than 28,000 members. He told me he learned valuable lessons from day one:

Early in my ministry at Mount Zion, I realized that relational leadership was essential to the survival of the church. Although families had controlled much of the direction of the church, it was important to embrace new ideas and innovative concepts of ministry from those who were coming in. The challenge, of course, was not alienating those who had been there before the church began to grow. You cannot leave those faithful saints behind. Often we pursue destiny and diminish history. Those folks had stories to share, wisdom to impart alongside the new creative approach to ministry. When you realize that everybody has a seat at the table of transition, you have a better chance of it coming to fruition. Some churches grow, but in actuality they are swelling. Wherever there is swelling there is infection. When you lead relationally you assure that the growth of the church is healthy.

Making Your Transition Relational

I have often been told that I have an old soul, but I never fully embraced that notion until I realized the older members at my first appointment found it an endearing quality. What I found this to mean there was that I was able to be in their presence and listen attentively to all they had to offer, even when I felt it might not work. This quality allowed me to make them feel valued as a part of the transition and new direction of the church. In all honesty, I really did enjoy being with them and learning the history firsthand. I learned of the joys and the sorrows, the good times and the not-so-good times throughout the church's existence. I was able to incorporate some of these stories into my sermons as a way of affirming all of the contributions the older members had made. I was also able to teach the newer members about their church's history. In an effort to further accentuate the relational aspect and not the generational, I created an opportunity during Black History Month for the older members to interact with the children and youth. Now, of course, this presented a challenge because it meant changing from what they had always done: one of the older members would read to the children about famous African Americans, and that was the extent of celebrating Black History Month at the church.

The idea I introduced allowed for more of the older members to share their own experiences during the Children's Moment part of the Sunday morning service. For each service I selected four of our older members to talk briefly about what life had been like for them when they were children and, more specifically, what the church had been like. Then I asked the children to write a short report on what they had heard and how they felt about it. During each Wednesday of Black History Month, the older members were our guests of honor at our Family Night Dinner program. The youth and young adults served the older members their meals, and after dinner the younger ones were encouraged to ask the older ones about their experiences. This was a powerful time of sharing, and it actually began relationship building.

17

The Young'uns and the Seasoned Saints

One of the other challenges at my first appointment was the fact that the city the church was in was growing quickly. New families were moving into the area, and this represented a threat to the older members who were already there. One of the concerns the older members expressed included the comment, "They won't be here long, just until their company moves them again." Another concern focused on the fact that the "new generation" would create all of these bills that the "older generation" would have to pay. At one point I found myself laughing when I realized I had said, "That's what we young'uns do." I had to remember that at thirty-six years old, I was considered a young'un myself. In light of this, I knew that in order to overcome this challenge, the new generation had to prove to the older generation that it was responsible, committed, and not simply caught up with having it and having it right now. Accomplishing this, however, was no easy task. One of the things we did was hold a Family Work Day to clean up the grounds and make necessary repairs. The young families organized it, planned the meals, and set it up for us to have a picnic after we finished our work. It was a blessed day in that we had nearly 100 percent participation, and the older members who took part in the event were extremely pleased by what they saw.

I can remember a particular instance during the Family Work Day involving a church pew, a young adult member, and an older member. It happened while we were cleaning out the basement of the church and discovered a pew down there. A group of the younger members wanted to simply toss it out, seeing no need to keep an old piece of church furniture. But one suggested we ask the older members about the pew before making any final decision. This was a small yet significant act. By deciding to ask an older member what to do, the younger members bridged a generational gap, probably without knowing it, which resulted in the older member they asked feeling respected for not only his knowledge about the pew but also the fact that his generation was responsible for the pew being there. Coincidentally, the younger member who had suggested we inquire about the pew was a relative of one of the older members who had been responsible for the pew.

The most beneficial aspect of this encounter was the fact that the younger members of the congregation were endearing themselves to the older members by showing respect for those items and traditions that had served to bring the church to its present place in the community. I could clearly see that the relational element of the transition in total was coming together. One of the components we often fail to address is that with transitional leadership, the fabric of the church community begins to transition as well. For instance, if the incoming leader is younger than the community, the membership will begin to transition to a younger population. Similarly, if the new leadership is older, the community will transition to an older spectrum of members. The challenge is to establish a medium wherein the generations are able to gel based on a relational perspective rather than one that simply considers age or tradition.

WITH TRANSITIONAL LEADERSHIP, THE FABRIC OF THE CHURCH COMMUNITY BEGINS TO TRANSITION AS WELL.

CHAPTER THREE

EXCUSE ME, WHERE'S THE BATHROOM?

Embarrassing but Necessary Questions: How to Build Community and Consensus

One of the most common mistakes most new leaders make is feeling as if they have to have all the answers. All too often when assuming their new positions, new leaders bring with them the baggage of past assignments. This baggage may include having been discounted or disrespected as a leader or repeatedly told, "I was here before you came, and I'll be here after you leave." Unfortunately, these experiences lend themselves to causing a new leader to formulate a mindset before understanding the culture. Just because there were people at the last assignment who did not support anything the leader presented does not mean there will be people at the current church who will operate in the same manner.

One of the most daunting tasks of all leaders is identifying a leadership style for themselves that will exemplify godly characteristics and move the mission forward. Initially, quite a few people will approach the new leader, promising full support and a willingness to do "whatever it takes." Unfortunately, it is hard to discern those who are sincere from those who simply want to position themselves to be major players for control's sake. That is, being the first to know so that they can manipulate the outcome.

IT IS HARD TO DISCERN THOSE WHO ARE SINCERE FROM THOSE WHO SIMPLY WANT TO POSITION THEMSELVES TO BE MAJOR PLAYERS FOR CONTROL'S SAKE.

The natural inclination is to do everything yourself in order to ensure information is being safeguarded and you as the new leader are maintaining control over the outcome. However, you will not last long trying to do it all alone. Such was the case with Moses until the meeting with his father-in-law, Jethro. We find in Exodus 18:17-27 how Jethro instructed Moses about the need to delegate.

Moses' father-in-law replied, "What you are doing is not good. You and these people who come to you will only wear yourselves out. The work is too heavy for you; you cannot handle it alone. Listen now to me and I will give you some advice, and may God be with you. You must be the people's representative before God and bring their disputes to him. Teach them the decrees and laws, and show them the way to live and the duties they are to perform. But select capable men from all the people—men who fear God, trustworthy men who hate dishonest gain—and appoint them as officials over thousands, hundreds, fifties and tens. Have them serve as judges for the people at all times, but have them bring every difficult case to you; the simple cases they can decide themselves. That will make your load lighter, because they will share it with you. If you do this and God so commands, you will be able to stand the strain, and all these people will go home satisfied."

Moses listened to his father-in-law and did everything he said. He

22

chose capable men from all Israel and made them leaders of the people, officials over thousands, hundreds, fifties and tens. They served as judges for the people at all times. The difficult cases they brought to Moses, but the simple ones they decided themselves.

Then Moses sent his father-in-law on his way, and Jethro returned to his own country.

It would be absolutely wonderful if we had the ability to choose a Dream Team every time we found ourselves in a new leadership position. However, reality dictates that we would miss it more times than we would hit it, and that is where our trust in God comes in. As we continue to work with God's people, God continually reminds us that God looks beyond our faults and sees our needs.

I can remember an encounter I had with an individual who had moved his membership from church to church and worked his way into key leadership positions with the sole intent of keeping the pastor from thinking that he or she had any authority to establish new initiatives. When I encountered this individual, I asked him to share with me the wisdom and insight he had gained as one of that church's few effective leaders. This approach did three things. First, it disarmed him with regard to thinking he and I were going to engage in a battle of wits. I already knew about his educational background and how he had dealt with pastors in the past, and I was ready to be the one to set the direction of our conversation. In other words, I knew with whom I was dealing. He had limited education; yet he was a very successful businessman in the community. Sadly, he constantly had to fight, argue, and defend what he had and hoped to attain. In his approach and conversations, he was what some might consider a little rough around the edges. What this meant for me was knowing that with him, everything was business: black-and-white, cut-and-dried, win or lose.

Second, my approach allowed me to present an opportunity for the member to relate to me as a mentor figure since he was a seasoned member of the church who was a respected leader. The danger with giving someone like him this opportunity is that if you are not mature enough to maintain the proper tension so as not to give away your authority, then the mentor figure will feel as if he or she is calling the shots. Maintaining the proper tension means that you ask for the meeting; you identify the date, time, and place; and you construct the agenda. While in the meeting, have your questions already formulated so that you can control the flow of the meeting and how much time is spent in the meeting. For instance, the mentor figure may just want to sit and talk. For you, this meeting will not be about information gathering or sharing. It will be about taking the temperature of the relationship or introducing a new initiative you need this individual to sign off on. You can conclude the meeting by saying, "I have one more question, and then I won't take up any more of your time." This allows you as the leader to maintain control of the time of the meeting, while giving the other person ample time to express himself or herself.

Finally, the approach I took with managing this individual put me in a position to foster a relationship with a person who could become an advocate rather than an adversary. Keep in mind that the only relationships that this gentleman apparently knew were ones that created an environment of knockdown, drag-out brawls. Using the process of inviting him to share his perspective with me in an encounter I could control gave me an opportunity to hear his objections, if any, before the issue went public. The new initiative you have planned for your church may not work even after you have spent time meeting with the individual you have invited to be a mentor figure. If this happens, you may need to create an opportunity for this person to tweak the initiative and make it his or her own. It also may not be the right time to introduce a new initiative, so you will need to be prepared to set it aside for a time.

FOSTER RELATIONSHIPS WITH PERSONS WHO MAY BECOME ADVOCATES RATHER THAN ADVERSARIES.

What I have found to be true about this particular process is that it is time consuming and often frustrating, and there is always the chance it may backfire. Nevertheless, enduring the process will do more for you in the long run in terms of learning how to read people, that is, discerning their spirit and being able to manage emotions, wills, and attitudes. It is true that expectations are placed upon the leader simply because of the responsibility that comes with the position. It is also true that there will be those who will not be supportive of the leadership change and will thereby position themselves to make the transition even more difficult than it has to be.

Asking Practical Yet Pertinent Questions

I once witnessed a situation wherein critical information was needed by a new pastor to make a decision about whether to repair or replace an organ in the church. The organ had been donated to the church by the family of a founding member, who was now deceased. This information alone should have immediately let the incoming leader know that, even if the organ could not be repaired, the pastor should not be the person to suggest having it replaced. A better approach would be for the pastor to call in a technician and then allow him or her to make an assessment and then make a professional recommendation to repair or replace the organ. This would be the practical and sensible solution. That, however, is not what happened in this incident. The church member who possessed this knowledge of the organ's history intentionally kept it from the new pastor. The pastor himself verbally suggested replacement based on the advice of the repair technician. Given the emotional attachment of the congregation to this organ, it would have been better for the pastor to have had the technician make a professional recommendation in writing to the trustee board—or anyone else other than himself.

The old saying about never assuming anything is a good one to remember when walking into new territory. Never assume that what looks obvious is the real deal. Never assume everyone who makes a statement with a smile has your best interest at heart. This is in no way to indicate that the majority will not support, protect, and help guide you. It is, however, the unfortunate reality.

Back to the incident of the organ. Had the pastor first asked his church members, "Tell me the history of this organ," the collective response would have eliminated any insincere or purposefully omitted information, and the problem would have been quelled before it ever began.

NEVER ASSUME THAT WHAT LOOKS OBVIOUS IS THE REAL DEAL. NEVER ASSUME EVERYONE WHO MAKES A STATEMENT WITH A SMILE HAS YOUR BEST INTEREST AT HEART. THIS IS IN NO WAY TO INDICATE THAT THE MAJORITY WILL NOT SUPPORT, PROTECT, AND HELP GUIDE YOU. IT IS, HOWEVER, THE UNFORTUNATE REALITY.

What we can learn from this is that regardless of how embarrassing a question may seem or how burning the desire is to give the impression you are knowledgeable, ask the question, "Excuse me, where's the bathroom?" Just be prepared that when you do, the person you ask may look at you like, "It's right there, can't you see it?" or "Can't you read? There's the sign right there." Although I use this humorous analogy of asking where the bathroom is, my major point is that a new leader cannot be embarrassed to ask seemingly simple questions. This act alone demonstrates to most, if not all, a willingness to be vulnerable and to create an opportunity for input. Too many leaders have walked into a broom closet thinking it was the bathroom and not realized someone was standing by watching and thinking, "If only you had asked." When we assume something is a bathroom just because it fits our definition of what the entrance to a bathroom should look like, we have basically formulated a conclusion based on an unsubstantiated observation. Similarly, just because we as leaders have a vision of what a new initiative should look like, does not mean we should not solicit input from those who know what that initiative should look like based on their understanding of the existing culture. A newcomer's perspective should be largely supported by testimonials of those who have been there.

DEMONSTRATE A WILLINGNESS TO BE VULNERABLE AND TO CREATE AN OPPORTUNITY FOR INPUT.

My father served in the United States Army for twenty-seven years, which included two tours in Vietnam. After he retired, he would frequently share stories with us (as much as he could, of course) about his time in Vietnam. What was surprising to me was that very little of his conversations dealt with the harm and devastation caused by the enemy. Instead, many of his stories dealt with his unit's new leader, a second lieutenant who had come straight from his commissioned officers training to the battlefield. Much of an officer's demonstrated proficiency is based on his or her intellectual ability to navigate simulated situations effectively, both in the classroom and on field maneuvers.

The operative word here is *simulated*. As we all have come to learn and know, theory oftentimes is no match for practical experience. Until the second lieutenant took command, he had not had the opportunity to gain the same experience with real warfare that my father's unit had already acquired. Ideally, a new officer and the battle-weary senior enlisted personnel develop a good working relationship, but this did not happen for my father's unit and its second lieutenant. My father, a senior enlisted member, told me that on more than one occasion when he tried to offer the new leader the benefit of his experience, he was given an order to simply obey orders.

The difficulty here is that as a member of the United States Army, my dad had taken an oath to follow orders, even when it conflicted with what he knew to be true. This was a challenge in that he knew following some orders could cause irreparable damage, devastation, and even death. Yet the second lieutenant was not asking the necessary but embarrassing questions my father felt he should. My father handled this situation by respecting his superiors but asking his peers and subordinates for their recommendations. In essence, what he was doing was building community, establishing trust, and, most importantly, letting the community know he genuinely cared for its welfare. The title of *leader* does not reflect competency or proficiency, nor does it constitute a guarantee for success. The lesson for us is that intellectual capital successfully partnered with human capital will ensure greater success. That is, *both and* versus *either-or*.

One of the exercises I have found to be very helpful is using a model of community building that asks small groups to select a vision area of the church and formulate ideas about how that vision will move the church in the direction of accomplishing its mission. Each group selects a topic, and a time frame is set for them to work on their vision area. The time frame can be one week, one month, or several months. The process includes think-tank gatherings, prayer, and formulating an outline or process to execute the group's ideas. Using this format allows the leader to visit each group and accomplish the following objective: observing group dynamics. This gives the leader an opportunity to understand how different people communicate. Knowing each individual's style of communication better equips the leader when it comes to having a conversation with the group members about a particular subject or asking them a simple question like "Where's the bathroom?" without them thinking the leader is totally inept or unqualified to occupy the position he or she has been called to.

I have witnessed colleagues who have refused to ask questions, and as a result the decisions they made cost them dearly in social capital. There was one situation in which the leader made a decision to take down pictures that were hanging in a hallway because the hallway needed to be repainted. After repainting the hallway, the leader decided to put the pictures in storage. Because my colleague did not want to appear incapable of making a decision as simple as moving pictures and painting a hallway, he failed to get the history of the pictures. After all, they were only pictures, and the hallway needed painting. What kind of leader would he be if he could not make a decision like that?

After a short period of time, when the congregation realized the pictures had not been returned to their rightful places on the hallway wall, a rift developed in the congregation. Several congregants became extremely upset and approached the leader about the matter. "Why did you move those pictures? Don't you know where they came from and how important they are to the history of this church?" And my favorite: "What committee did you check with?" Granted, the pictures may have needed to be moved. However, something that initially appeared to be relatively minor turned into something that was more trouble than it was worth. Had the leader not been too embarrassed to ask a simple question, "Excuse me, can you tell me about these pictures?" or "These are absolutely wonderful! Can you tell me where they came from?" then the entire situation more than likely would have turned out differently. By giving the questions an excited emphasis, my colleague would have been able to endear himself to the church because of his inferred affinity to pictures that undoubtedly meant a lot to the congregation. Necessary but embarrassing questions can prove to be stepping-stones instead of land mines. If the right question is not asked in the right manner, then the situation can be blown out of proportion.

On another occasion, I personally witnessed what could happen if a necessary but embarrassing question was not asked. There was a member in one of my congregations whose gift was interior decorating. She wanted to place sheer window treatments over some windows, and she asked me if that would be okay. I said, "Of course." She proceeded to purchase the material with her own money, sew the window treatments with her own equipment, and put them in place on her own time. After the project had been completed, I acknowledged it and thanked her publicly for a job well done. Prior to this, I had been alerted to the fact that some members were not happy that I had given permission to an individual to complete this project. What I found to be the core issue was the fact that, unbeknownst to me, a group called the Beautification Committee was already in place to handle projects like this. In my excitement to have a member volunteer to do something, and not wanting to appear as if I needed permission to do something as mundane as covering windows, I failed to ask a necessary but embarrassing question: "Is there a team already in place for this?"

These questions are necessary because they demonstrate your ability as a leader to stay connected to the team and to foster teamwork. These questions do not make it appear as though you are abdicating responsibility or incapable of making simple decisions. As the leader, you must not become overly excited or so caught up that process is thrown out the window. Process includes asking these simple but necessary questions: Who? What? When? Where? and Why?

QUESTIONS DEMONSTRATE YOUR ABILITY AS A LEADER TO STAY CONNECTED TO THE

TEAM AND TO FOSTER TEAMWORK.

Dealing with the *W*s

When we ask *Who?* we are asking who else is supportive of the idea that is being presented. This will give you a better understanding of the segment of the community that is behind the initiative. It will also present you with an opportunity to see who the presenter is connected to.

When we ask the question *What?* we are asking, "What is it exactly that you want to do, what is required to get it done, and what is expected of me as the leader?"

The question *When?* defines the time period during which all activity around this initiative is to take place. This ensures that other initiatives or ministries are not neglected, and it prevents the perception of favoritism. It also helps keep new initiatives from being highlighted at the same time, which would cause unnecessary and unhealthy competition between ministries.

Where? defines the parameters to be used as the new initiative is introduced to the congregation, parameters that include both inside the church and outside of the church. It is important to understand the exposure the church has out in the community. In this instance, a necessary but embarrassing question might be, "Will this initiative require input from the outside community?" For instance, what resources would the outside community be required to provide? These could include, but not be limited to, the use of buildings or other community resources. Another necessary question to ask would be, "Will this initiative involve other churches and their leadership?"

Why? asks the question of whether this initiative fits the mission and vision of the church. It asks the question as to whether the

31

initiative is solely for the purpose of self-aggrandizement. Furthermore, it gives the leader an opportunity to discern whether the initiative is solely for the purpose of serving a select group, or whether it will serve the entire community.

All too often a new leader will simply say yes to a new idea or initiative to placate those presenting the idea. This is detrimental because it opens the way for others to present good ideas rather than God ideas. A good idea is one that tickles the ears, pleases the flesh, and is temporary at best in its existence. A God idea is one that has come to fruition after studying and meditating on God's word to see how the idea can be used to bring others to Christ. Additionally, prayerful consideration is given to ensure the idea brings glory to God and not to a particular person or only a few individuals. With a God idea, the entire community is served for the glory of God.

A GOOD IDEA IS ONE THAT TICKLES THE EARS, PLEASES THE FLESH, AND IS TEMPORARY IN ITS EXISTENCE. A GOD IDEA IS ONE THAT HAS COME TO FRUITION AFTER STUDYING AND MEDITATING ON GOD'S WORD TO SEE HOW THE IDEA CAN BE USED TO BRING OTHERS TO CHRIST. ADDITIONALLY, PRAYERFUL CONSIDERATION IS GIVEN TO ENSURE THE

IDEA BRINGS GLORY TO GOD
AND NOT TO A PARTICULAR
PERSON OR ONLY A FEW IN-
DIVIDUALS. WITH A GOD
IDEA, THE ENTIRE COMMUNI-
TY IS SERVED FOR THE
GLORY OF GOD.

CHAPTER FOUR

ARE WE RELATED?

Establishing Connectedness: Celebrating Each
Other's Gifts and Abilities

One of the more amusing moments during my first ministry appointment occurred on the church's "Family Sunday." On this day we encouraged families to sit together, and after the service we had a picnic on the grounds. At the time, this church was about one hundred members strong, small enough for everyone to know each other. As I made my way through the crowd, moving from family to family, I began to notice who was related to whom. I had had no idea there were so many who were connected as extended families within the congregation. What was even more amusing was that they talked to me about each other without giving me any indication they were related. Praise God I had the good sense not to comment one way or the other but to simply listen and remain pastoral in my responses!

My challenge was navigating the different familial dynamics that existed because the family members were in key leadership positions. For instance, the congregation was primarily controlled by the immediate members of one family, who allowed limited participation by extended members of the same family. That is to say, the mother was in a key leadership position in one area, while her nephew held the number-two leadership position in another ministry area.

Sticks and Stones Will Break Your Bones, and Words Will Often Hurt You

It is extremely important to remember that you never know whom you are talking to and who is related to whom. This ambiguity should cause the new leader to always focus on accentuating the gifts of everyone and leading in such a manner that the community is able to see how these gifts work well together. We learn of this approach in 1 Corinthians 12:4-7, where the apostle Paul tells us that "there are different kinds of spiritual gifts, but the same Spirit is the source of them all. There are different kinds of service, but we serve the same Lord. God works in different ways, but it is the same God who does the work in all of us" (NLT). God has given each of us a spiritual gift, and it is meant to be used to help the entire church.

You never know whom you are talking to and who is related to whom.

The downside to leading a church in which everyone is related is that if there is any dissention between the interconnected families, it can tremendously impact the rate of progress in building a healthy community. The most important thing the leader can do is maintain a position of neutrality yet firmness in establishing how the families will interact with one another. This will oftentimes include mediating passionate conversations that could become personal and destructive. We've all grown up hearing the saying, "Sticks and stones may break my bones, but words will never hurt me." However, what we know to be true is that sticks and stones will indeed break our bones, and words can most definitely hurt us.

The most important thing the leader can do is maintain a position of neutrality yet firmness in establishing how the

FAMILIES WILL INTERACT WITH ONE ANOTHER.

Research has shown that a well-defined leadership selection process may not guarantee success, but it will certainly provide a solid platform from which good leaders within the church can be selected. Three steps in the process have proven to be effective. They are as follows. First, the candidate for a leadership position needs to take a spiritual gifts inventory test to identify his or her gifts and area of passion in the ministry. One of my mentors told me this helps weed out those who are simply seeking power positions from those who are willing to bring passion for their calling to the table. I shared with him my feeling that, honestly, everyone in the church was seeking the power positions because they were not familiar with me and wanted to make sure they protected their church.

RESEARCH HAS SHOWN THAT A WELL-DEFINED LEADERSHIP SELECTION PROCESS MAY NOT GUARANTEE SUCCESS, BUT IT WILL CERTAINLY PROVIDE A SOLID PLATFORM FROM WHICH GOOD LEADERS WITHIN THE CHURCH CAN BE SELECTED.

The second step centers on examining the candidate's previous areas of service and how well he or she did in them. My mentor said that this is a way of exposing either the effectiveness or ineffectiveness of the potential leader. For instance, did the committee or team this person led display fruitfulness? Did the ministry this person led encourage others to be a part of it or shy away from it? How well did this person relate not only to his or her team members but also to other leaders and those in the community in general? Is this person one who sows seeds of discord, or is he or she able to create synergy to promote a team of healthy individuals working together to move the vision forward? These are the questions that have to be answered.

The third step in the process is discerning the candidate's demonstrated level of spiritual maturity. Spiritual maturity is that level of behavior that allows us to interact with one another in a constructive, not destructive, manner. Interaction within a community is destructive when egos, attitudes, wills, and emotions are put before God's desire for harmony. Everyone must be in a position to support the new leadership in such a manner that harmony thrives or is evident, even in the midst of uncertainty, confusion, and, yes, chaos. This is a monumental issue when the leader is unable to create an atmosphere in which individuals are willing to reason with one another. In situations like these the question "Can we all just get along?" becomes the mantra of the day.

The natural inclination is to dispense with individuals who create challenge and appear to present themselves as not being team players. But if we do not try to understand their core issue as to why they are not supportive of the initiative on the table, then we give them license to become disconnected from the team and the vision and then to infect the rest of the community with their disgruntled behavior and negative conversation. We put ourselves and the community at risk of being hurt by their words. But when we take the stance that we are all related, are all part of the family, we are able to position ourselves to maintaining a connection. A premature disconnection would keep us from gaining valuable information from the people who are causing the turmoil. This information might include who else they are connected to and if their position of disagreement is singularly focused or more widespread than originally anticipated. Finally, it causes the leader to ask and then answer the question as to whether there is an opportunity to transform this adversary into an ally.

THE NATURAL INCLINATION IS TO DISPENSE WITH INDIVIDUALS WHO CREATE CHALLENGE AND APPEAR TO PRESENT THEMSELVES AS NOT BEING TEAM PLAYERS. BUT IF WE DO NOT TRY TO UNDERSTAND THEIR CORE ISSUE AS TO WHY THEY ARE NOT SUPPORTIVE OF THE INITIATIVE ON THE TABLE, THEN WE GIVE THEM LICENSE TO BECOME DISCONNECTED FROM THE TEAM AND THE VISION AND THEN TO INFECT THE REST OF THE COMMUNITY WITH THEIR DISGRUNTLED BEHAVIOR AND NEGATIVE CONVERSATION.

There Is No I in Team

Growing up, my brother and I were constantly engaged in sibling rivalry. This oftentimes resulted in wrestling and even a few punches being thrown. However, we understood that no matter how angry we were, if we harmed one another, we would answer to a higher power—that power being our mom. We were clear about the fact that we were family and that we worked through our disagreements. That same understanding must be established as the mode of operation in the life of any membership that desires to prosper. All too often the mind-set of some individuals is "we can do what we want, however we want, regardless of whom it affects." So then the question becomes "How do we create a sense of family and a community of genuine concern for our neighbor?" After all, the Bible says, "'You shall love your neighbor as yourself.' There is no other commandment greater than these" (Mark 12:31 NRSV). God clearly teaches us how to love one another as God has loved us. What this means for us is that we have to continue to look beyond each other's faults and see the good. We have to exhibit above-normal levels of patience with one another, and we have to understand that perfection is not necessarily getting it right at the expense of unity and morale but getting it done in the right way to promote greater unity and to celebrate the gifts everyone brings.

PERFECTION IS NOT NECESSARILY GETTING IT RIGHT AT THE EXPENSE OF UNITY AND MORALE BUT GETTING IT DONE IN THE RIGHT WAY TO PROMOTE GREATER UNITY AND TO CELEBRATE THE GIFTS EVERYONE BRINGS.

At my first appointment, I was always amazed at how excited the congregation would be when we would have our church picnics. Everyone would be assigned a particular dish to bring, and conversation would ensue about how delicious someone's macaroni and cheese was or how good someone else's homemade pound cake tasted. As I moved from group to group sampling all the food, I was happy to be a part of that church family. But the questions that kept tugging at my heart were "What can I as the leader do to encourage this same joy and passion the members have for preparing delectable dishes around doing God's business and moving the ministry to the next level? What can be done to keep this same sense of family and camaraderie when dealing with the tough issues?" At one picnic, after my third helping of banana pudding, it occurred to me that more consideration needed to be given to partnering people based on giftedness and not skill set. I realized that even if an individual is a professional in any given area the church needs expertise in, he or she may not possess the right personality trait to be a part of that team. We have all experienced those individuals who are experts in a field but grossly lack the compassion and spirit necessary to create an environment that celebrates everyone's gifts.

The second thing that occurred to me is that we needed to be more intentional about celebrating the small victories. As leaders, we must not be so focused on the big things we want to happen that we forget to celebrate everything else that enables success. Even if the desired goal was not accomplished, it is important to celebrate the hard work the team put into trying to get to that goal. In the midst of this merriment we should reset our objectives and be ready to start anew. Our celebration should focus more on how everyone's gifts came together to move the ball down the field instead of on an individual's effort to score the winning touchdown. In addition to being a morale booster, a celebration affords the opportunity to create a high level of excitement and a greater commitment to the task. For instance, going back to the church picnic, people wanted to be in the sack race, the three-legged race, the softball match—they enjoyed the games. I noticed the high level of competitiveness and overall joy

41

of just being a part of those games. So I needed to transfer the same dynamics that occurred at the church picnic to the church council meeting. The challenge was not so great, which I think was primarily due to the fact that I had a sufficient number of members to select from. I did not start out that way, however, and work had to be done to create a critical mass of people with differing age levels, education, and socioeconomic backgrounds.

AS LEADERS, WE MUST NOT BE SO FOCUSED ON THE BIG THINGS WE WANT TO HAPPEN THAT WE FORGET TO CELEBRATE EVERYTHING ELSE THAT ENABLES SUCCESS.

To create the critical mass, most, if not all, of my attention was given to ensuring that the worship style was germane to the community in which the church was located. This meant paying particular attention to the preaching style and the music. Upon my arrival, I discovered that the church had two worship services, and the style of worship was traditional at both. However, the church had more individuals who preferred a more contemporary service to a traditional one. I discovered this from general conversations with members about why they would attend other churches instead of the one, our church, located just a couple of miles from their home. They would explain, "The music was livelier and more up-to-date" or, "The preacher wasn't boring and didn't put me to sleep." They also commented that other churches had more activities for their children. You see, most of these people had young families and were nontraditional; had limited time they wanted to devote to spiritual formation, or to church for that matter; and needed to be addressed in an unconventional manner. Technology, brevity, and a high level of return on their investment were paramount concerns.

With this information I introduced a concept that allowed for two different worship styles with a periodic combination of the two, thus creating a blended family. As many are aware, the more worship services you offer, the more communities you create within that one structure. Therefore, careful attention must be given to consistent, regular church picnic opportunities, or a family reunion; that is to say, aunts, uncles, and cousins coming together to become reacquainted with one another, thus declaring, "We are related." Putting it another way, the traditionalists and the nontraditionalists are able to understand that they serve the one God for the same purpose of creating family. After the church made the necessary adjustments, worship attendance tripled in about six months and membership doubled in twelve months.

We Are Family

We all need to remember *who* we are and *whose* we are. We are children of God, and we belong to God. So then, how does that influence our behavior? Mama always said, "If you can't say something nice, then don't say anything at all." My response is, "Easier said than done." All too often we are provoked at the most inopportune times. It can be when we are stressed from the activities of earlier in the day, or when we are just having a bad day and then have to come to church. And as many of us are aware, it only takes one more thing to cause us to lay our religion down. As leaders, it is imperative that we remember to always conduct ourselves in a manner that shows who we are and whose we are. This means that our actions, our conversation, and our attitude all must reflect that God is in control of us and the situation. It may mean counting to 10 or even to 110. But the end result should be one where the sense of family is protected and an environment of understanding is the norm.

OUR ACTIONS, OUR CONVERSATION, AND OUR ATTITUDE ALL MUST REFLECT THAT GOD IS IN CONTROL OF US AND THE SITUATION. IT MAY MEAN COUNTING TO 10 OR EVEN TO 110.

In order to be prepared at all times to respond to behaviors and conversations that seek to destroy the family and the community, a good leader is extremely intentional about placing himself or herself in a time-out mode. The normal understanding of being in time-out is that you are the one who has committed an infraction that was outside the boundaries, guidelines, and expectations with regard to conducting yourself well in the community. But in this sense, you are merely being intentional about protecting your time that can be spent in prayer, meditation, or simply just sitting and staring at a blank wall. A self-imposed time-out will allow you to clear your mind and get ready for the next client.

I can remember when I was in retail banking and had to assist customers with their banking needs. I had to learn that regardless of how many customers I assisted who had the same complaint, I always needed to treat the next one as if that person was the first customer I was helping that day. Similarly, in the church ten people will invariably come to you as the leader with the exact same complaint, as if each is the only one who has noticed a problem with something. Depending upon your response, both verbal and non-verbal, the church family will either be strengthened or be tossed into turmoil. For example, if you respond with a sincere, "Thank you so much. Several other members have noticed it as well, and we are looking into it," then you will have exhibited a leadership trait that serves to strengthen the family. Conversely, if your response is "Do I look like I'm the one who handles that?" then you have just lessened your ability to strengthen the community through spiritual maturity. Even though it may not be your job, as the Sister Sledge song goes, "We are family." Growing up in my house, even if it wasn't your toy on the floor, you picked it up and put it where it belonged. Even if it wasn't your turn to wash the dishes, if the person responsible for that job was ill, absent, or just plain forgot, you carried out the responsibility. In this sense, handling multiple complaints, even if they are about things that are not your responsibility, as if this is the first time you have heard the complaint provides an opportunity to educate, inform, and, most importantly, influence behavior in such a way that everyone in the church has a strong sense of family and exhibits a desire to accomplish the objectives.

In his book *Martin Luther King, Jr., on Leadership: Inspiration and Wisdom for Challenging Times*, Donald T. Phillips highlights what else you have to gain from patient listening in chapter 13, "Understand Human Nature":

> Leaders must also understand human nature so that they may better understand themselves. By having an awareness of why people behave the way they do, a good leader will be able to apply that knowledge to his or her own specific performance and interactions. The most frequent result of such self-analysis causes the leader to become more compassionate and more empathetic. When leaders display such tendencies toward followers, it almost always results in greater acceptance and genuine affection for the leader. (Phillips [New York: Warner, 1998], 270)

A congregation is best served by a leader who is able to inspire and empower the family to pitch in and get it done. Just like at the end of a family reunion or church picnic, when all of the fun has ended, everyone is full of delicious food, contests are over, and congratulations have been given, everyone has come together to clean up and look ahead to the next time. Likewise, with each passing day, the new leader must be prepared to clean up and get ready for the next day.

Just like at the end of a family reunion or church picnic, when all of the fun has ended, everyone is full of delicious food, contests are over, and congratulations have been given, everyone has come together to clean up and look ahead to the next time. Likewise, with each passing day, the new leader must be prepared to clean up and get ready for the next day.

Are We There Yet?

How to Establish Mutually Acceptable Goals and Outline the Process to Measure Progress

Every year our parents would plan our family summer vacation. We would always go to the same location: Top Sail Beach, North Carolina. As children, the excitement my brother and I felt was predicated on the fact that, not only were we going to the beach, but we were also actually taking a vacation. You see, we were not wealthy, but our parents saw to it that we had an opportunity to experience time away as a family. So our excitement was fueled by the mystique created as a result of our not being a part of our parents' planning session, even though we always went to the same place. I must admit it is funny thinking back now on my mother asking, "Where would you boys like to go for your summer vacation?" even though our wish would not be granted. At the time, we were excited simply to be asked that question. We had no idea that, regardless of our response, Top Sail Beach would be the answer.

Mom would make bologna-with-cheese sandwiches in preparation for the trip. We would also have fried chicken and potato salad. She would instruct us to go get our swimming trunks and towels, and Dad would make sure the car was serviced, gassed up, and ready to go. Mom would check that the coolers were still intact. You remember those Styrofoam coolers that would squeak the entire ride if they were not positioned properly? They would also crumble into a million pieces if they were not handled properly. Once we had the car packed and everyone on board, we would say a quick prayer and hit the road. For the next two-and-a-half hours, my brother and I would sit in the back seat and play "That's My Car" and fight with each other. Our mom would warn us that if we did not stop fighting she would tell our dad to turn the car around and we would go home. At the time, we did not understand that turning around was not an option because we had come too far to turn back. The mere threat would make us straighten up, stop fighting, and look forward to reaching our destination. When we became bored with playing games and realized that fighting each other was not an option, we would begin posing the tedious question every child on a long car trip asks: "Are we there yet?"

Taking the Fear Out of the Journey

I believe all can agree that when taking a long trip, everyone wants to get there, but no one wants to make the journey. Patience is short, excitement is high, skepticism is pervasive, and doubt is debilitating. Are we really going to be able to do this? We cannot seriously consider doing it, can we? Such questions come up when embarking upon a new adventure or when change is so monumental it paralyzes a community or when it comes to embracing new and more innovative ideas. It is an indisputable fact that when there is a change in leadership, there will be a change in policy and procedure. The unknown is what invariably pushes the existing community into a state of frenzy and fear. Before there is an opportunity to explain your position, you as the new leader will be immediately placed on the defensive in that the existing community's perception of who you are, the expectations of what you will do, and whatever other preconceived notions exist will become its reality. The community knows change is going to occur, it just does not know what that change means for it, and it perceives that the change will be uncomfortable. The new leader must seize every available opportunity in the beginning to set expectations and to invite as many of those who are desirous of being included to be a part of planning the trip and helping to prepare for the journey. This course of action will afford you as the new leader the opportunity to personally let everyone know you are all taking a family trip and each person has a responsibility to make sure you reach your destination.

WHEN THERE IS A CHANGE IN LEADERSHIP, THERE WILL BE A CHANGE IN POLICY AND PROCEDURE.

Sometimes getting to our destination is extremely difficult, not to mention the fact that even as pastors, we may not be clear about where we are going. What we do know is even in times of uncertainty we must continue to depend upon God. The best example of this can be found in the story of Abram, wherein Abram is called to leave a place of familiarity to go to a place of promise. "The LORD had said to Abram, 'Leave your native country, your relatives, and your father's family, and go to the land that I will show you. I will make you into a great nation. I will bless you and make you famous, and you will be a blessing to others. I will bless those who bless you and curse those who treat you with contempt. All the families on earth will be blessed through you'" (Gen. 12:1-3 NLT).

One of the first things I did at my first appointment was to schedule a meeting with each family or member of the church. I called them "Pastor Chats" and held them for a one-month period. These meetings included the children and youth of each family because I wanted to take advantage of the opportunity to interact with the youngest members of the congregation and find out as much about them, from them, as I could. Some of this information included where they went to school, who they were friends with at the church, and what would make church fun for them. Meeting with everyone was not a monumental task because the membership was less than one hundred. I asked everyone I met three questions: (1) "How long have you been a member of the church?"; (2) "What is the vision of the church?"; and (3) "If you were the pastor, what would you do?" This strategy afforded me an opportunity to get to know the members of the congregation as well as personally inform them of any changes that might occur. The questions I asked gave them an opportunity to be a part of planning the family trip, that is, preparing our vision statement and providing their input as to where we would go as a family, that is, strengthening the focus of the membership. I was intentional about making notes during each visit so that I could revisit the conversations later. Another important element of these Pastor Chats was hearing from members about whether they wanted to take a trip, much less go to the beach. In other words, did they have an understanding of the importance of having a vision statement for the church, and were they willing to participate in writing one? (I must add here that none of the people I met with knew the church's vision or even had a clue that there was a need for one. However, all were able to tell me what they would do if they were the pastor!)

The next step was to have the members agree to a family-night dinner so that I could share the results of my conversations with them. It would be a potluck dinner, and a team was put together to coordinate the logistics. Each family was grouped by the first letter of their last name and assigned a dish to bring. This ensured we would not have too much of any one item. Activities and games were arranged for the children and nursery service was available as well. The dinner was open to everyone, which allowed for those who had not signed up for a Pastor Chat to attend and perhaps schedule one at the dinner. I made sure a registration sheet was available, and five individuals and three families signed up for a Pastor Chat to be held later. This still did not capture everyone in the membership, but I did not continue to try to convince everyone to participate. I simply moved forward with those who had signed up.

The dinner was a huge success. Besides the food being absolutely awesome, the fellowship was great. Of the one-hundred-person membership, approximately sixty attended the dinner. The fellowship hall was small, so we had people everywhere. The children created a picnic area by spreading blankets on the floor and eating their meals there. As I visited each group that had gathered for the dinner, I thanked them for coming and expressed how excited I was to be a part of such a wonderful family. I was intentional about using the word *family* because that was the environment I was trying to create. Furthermore, I wanted them to understand that everything relating to this ministry moving forward from this point on would be more about "we" than "me." In other words, the congregation would have to agree to come together to establish mutually acceptable goals and objectives. After I had had an opportunity to visit with everyone in the room and it appeared as though most families had finished their meal, I asked everyone to focus their attention on the large pads of paper I had set up on easels.

Write the Vision

To prepare for my presentation at the dinner, I had recorded on the pads of paper, under the appropriate headings, everyone's responses to the questions I had asked during my Pastor Chats: "How long have you been a member?" "What is the vision of the church?" and "What would you do if you were the pastor?" I had to edit some of the responses so as not to embarrass anyone. I also positioned the responses on each pad, lining them up in separate columns, so that they would lead us to concurring we needed to schedule some time together in the near future to agree on a single vision for the church and come up with a vision statement, a mission statement, and a set of core values. I would like to note here that I used the paper-and-pen method and not a PowerPoint presentation because I wanted to be able to engage the group from the very beginning by asking for volunteers. The volunteers would be responsible for writing on the pads any additional thoughts and striking those thoughts we agreed needed to be removed. To begin the session, I reminded everyone that we wanted to be done by 8:30 p.m. and asked whether, if we did not finish that evening, we could decide on a time to come together again to conclude our discussion. They agreed we could meet again at a later date. Remember now, one of the objectives was to get them to want to come together again, so when this went as smoothly as it did, I had to calm myself down so as to not become too euphoric about the rest of the session going as smoothly. After all, we were embarking upon one element that is present in every single transition of leadership, and that was the element of inevitable change. To put it plainly, the next phase of the session would open the door for someone to utter the "But we've never done it that way before" response.

Some of the people who had participated in the Pastor Chats had been members of the church for at least ten or fifteen years, and they shared some of their fond memories. They also shared horror stories of leadership gone wrong. They expressed their fears, and I had to keep reminding myself to be extra sensitive to their concerns at all times. Being sensitive did not mean we would forego visioning for the next level of ministry; it simply meant that I had to always create opportunities for individuals to be a part of the plan from day one. It also meant that instead of driving 60 miles per hour while on this journey, I would have to slow it down to perhaps 45 or 50 miles per hour so as not to frighten everyone on our family trip. There would need to be ample small-group conversations facilitated by members of the church. I would need to position myself to be in more of a listening posture as often as possible.

This family-night dinner presented me with the opportunity to model how to facilitate a meeting and to introduce myself as one who truly wanted to hear from the congregation and involve them in the transition. I started the sharing session with another thank-you to those who had signed up for the Pastor Chats and a thank-you to those who had not had an opportunity to participate in them but had come to the dinner and were prepared to share. I then explained that I had captured on the pads their responses to the Pastor Chat questions and wanted to share them with everyone. But before we could start, I would need to ask for some help. I would need someone to help me make sure any additional comments made that evening were written down on the pads, and, if I had not clearly stated something that had been shared previously, to let me know so the volunteer could write it more accurately. Regardless of how miniscule this task may seem, my intentional use of the word *help* gained me valuable mileage. Asking for help did not make me appear weak; rather, it made me able to demonstrate my willingness to engage others. Care must be given to ensuring that engaging others is done in a way that is genuine and authentic.

Don't Forget the Follow-up

After a couple of individuals agreed to help me, I proceeded with the time of sharing, restating the categories and the shared responses. I then asked if there was anyone in attendance who had participated in the Pastor Chats but wanted to add something now. I also asked for participation from those who had not taken part in the Pastor Chats but wanted to share. A few did, and each began with an apology for not having been able to participate in the Pastor Chats. This step was important because it allowed me to gauge my audience: those who cared and were sensitive to not being able to fulfill the request and those who simply did not do it and felt, "That's that, and don't ask me any questions about it!" As the agreed-upon time to end the evening approached, I began to frame the discussion of the evening as the beginning of a series of gatherings that would allow us to come together to continue planning our trip. We would spend time coming up with a mission statement, a vision statement, and a set of core values. After we crafted the vision and mission statements and agreed upon the core values, we would come together to establish goals and objectives, agree upon how to measure accomplishment, and later, most importantly, celebrate them. When I asked if everyone was in agreement with the plan, the response was not as robust as I would have hoped for, but enough people said, "Okay," for us to move forward.

I closed the session by asking if anyone had anything they wanted to share before we concluded. One of the older members raised his hand and said he had a comment. The gentleman cleared his throat slightly, folded his arms tightly across his chest, looked over his reading glasses, and stated loudly, "Pastor, I hope you are not taking us through all of this to come up with all of these newfangled ideas just to tell somebody about Jesus! We need someone to teach us and preach good. We don't need a bunch of stuff to do, and we certainly don't need anyone putting us into debt! I hope you hear me, Preacher!" When he finished, some gasped, others laughed, and still others had a look of "I can't believe he said that!" I must be honest. It was at this moment that I saw all of my best laid-out plans going down the drain. I had to think quickly: "What do I do with this?" I immediately began to laugh, even though on the inside I was embarrassed, angry, and wondering to myself why he had waited until now to say this. He could have said it in my office in a private meeting with me. But instead, he had decided to wait until we were in front of all of these people and at the end of what I had considered a successful first visioning session.

After the laughter stopped I said, "Well, from what I've learned in my short time with you, you all tell people about Jesus extremely well. We just need to figure out how to get the story out to those who have never heard it before and get them excited about coming here to see Jesus in action. That's all I am trying to do. But I can truly appreciate what you have shared with us tonight, and I would love to spend some more time with you to hear more so that, while we're planning on what to do next, we're careful to pay attention to your thoughts." After that, I thanked everyone again for a wonderful family-night dinner and told them that I would see them on Sunday. I made sure to thank the older member who had shared his thoughts, and I reiterated my desire to spend more time with him to more fully capture his concerns. He still had a stern look on his face as if to say, "I meant what I said!" Nevertheless, I kept a smile on my face.

Later that night, as I was going back over everything that had taken place, I had to conclude that, for the most part, it had been a very successful evening. The attendance was great, the food was good, and the people participated. I even heard a few say we needed to do this more often than once a year. The following Sunday, I thanked everyone again for a wonderful time on Wednesday evening, and I shared the excitement I felt about us getting together again to make a plan to reach more people for Jesus. There was clapping from the congregation, and a few said, "Amen!" I then told the congregation that our faith walk with Christ was a journey, and we needed to make sure as many people as possible wanted to take the journey with us. We needed to decide how we were going to do it and what things we would like to see when our job was done. In other words, when we arrived there should be no one asking the question, "Are we there yet?"

CHAPTER SIX

I NEED YOU, YOU NEED ME

Highlighting Interdependence and Establishing
Process for Support and Accountability

The apostle Paul helps us understand that doing God's work is going to take all of us: "For as we have many members in one body, but all the members do not have the same function, so we, *being* many, are one body in Christ, and individually members of one another" (Rom. 12:4-5 NKJV). We must not continue to work in vacuums or as individuals. We must come together as the family of God in order to do what God requires of us. We all have something to offer and must create an environment where people feel welcomed to share their thoughts and ideas. It will take all of us working, praying, crying, praising, and worshiping God in order to effectively be a part of building the Kingdom.

It is unfortunate that prior to the recent economic upheaval there was a tremendous amount of individualism and insensitivity to the needs of the greater community. However, the housing bust and economic challenges that plagued the country beginning in 2006 forced families to come together to survive. Younger and upwardly mobile individuals found themselves having to move in with their parents after companies downsized and eliminated positions. With the rising cost of commodities, neighbors began borrowing sugar, bread, and butter from each other, as they had done in days of old. There was a new forced level of interdependence, given the lack of resources needed to meet individual needs. To put it plainly, communities found themselves needing each other in order to survive.

Getting Connected

Throughout history we have accounts of individuals who have made decisions in a vacuum. There was no sense of collaboration, conversation, or cooperation, and as a result, the decision oftentimes served the individual rather than the good of the community. When shortcuts are taken to reach a decision about a particular goal, objective, or direction, then the most important elements are neglected and frequently eliminated eventually from the DNA of a particular group. For instance, the president of the United States must rely on information from his cabinet members and others around him to come to a decision about matters that affect an entire nation. While we highlight the effect his decision has on the nation, more specifically, the impact directly affects those closest to him and those who support him. The president's decision-making process must lend itself to the incorporation of comments and suggestions from those with whom he does not necessarily agree. Nevertheless, he needs them, and they need him to continue to move the country forward.

A similar political culture exists within the church. Like our country's president, a church leader must be able to blend differing views to arrive at a decision to move the church forward. This is something new leaders will encounter sooner rather than later. The art here is to possess the ability to weave together differing opinions and at the same time still exhibit the characteristics of a leader who is decisive and can make decisions that benefit the community; that is to say, the leader does not appear as needing the input of others but as desiring the input so that consideration can be given to the different components that go into the decision.

A CHURCH LEADER MUST BE ABLE TO BLEND DIFFERING VIEWS TO ARRIVE AT A DECI-

SION TO MOVE THE CHURCH FORWARD.

One experience I had with collaborative decision making involved creating an additional worship service to attract the young adult population. Before asking for a vote, I polled the congregation to get its opinion on starting a contemporary worship service. Of course the members expressed a myriad of views, but unfortunately there were more negative comments than positive ones. I had to understand what was behind the negative responses. In addition to the obvious—changes were on the way—I needed to get to the core issue. So I spent time with just a few of those who did not think it was a good idea to start a service to attract younger people. One of the perspectives these members shared was a feeling that the church would be spending additional money to attract those who were not going to give any money or be committed to staying and supporting the ministry of the church. I found this to be interesting because the contemporary service would not require extra funds. The additional service would, in fact, bring in more money. However, the comment about the transiency of the younger crowd was valid. These individuals worked for companies that transferred them almost as frequently as The United Methodist Church transfers its pastors.

In The United Methodist Church, the pastors are itinerant, which means that they are subject to being transferred to another church after a period of time. This process keeps the local church in a state of transition. The most common practice is to transfer a pastor after two or three years, which positions local congregations to have an "us and them" mentality. The frequent pastor turnovers create a problem for the new leader in that they make the congregation's survival dependent on its own resources and ability to sustain a community. In spite of the fact that the bishop makes the appointment, the atmosphere in the church has already been set for the expectation of a new transition every two or three years. So then, each new pastor has to figure out how to operate in a manner that will say to the congregation that he or she plans to serve the people for longer than the time to which they were accustomed.

Relationship Building Versus Kingdom Building

A tremendous challenge for a new pastor is that more time has to be given to building relationships than casting a vision for kingdom building. Depending upon the number of leadership transitions that have occurred previously, the incoming pastor can face an insurmountable challenge from the congregation when it comes to truly positioning the congregation to feel as though the members need each other. It must also be noted that a congregational community consists of individuals of varying beliefs and values who provide an opportunity for extremely diverse opinions and ideas to be introduced on any given subject. So then, how does the new leader move to create an atmosphere wherein, despite opposing views, people are encouraged to express those views and be open to further discussion? The answer is not clearly set in black-and-white. While discussion does not guarantee a solution or a coming to an agreement, it does provide the opportunity to hear what others are thinking. Contrary to popular opinion, discussion is an extremely common element of the decision-making process. Granted, if careful attention is not given to this discussion, the situation could become a free-for-all, with everyone talking and no one listening. Therefore, at the beginning of any discussion session, it is extremely important to set parameters that are inclusive with regard to the number of speakers allowed who will be in support of and against a particular topic.

Celebrating Each Other's Gifts

In the life of the church, while one person has to serve as the leader and ultimately cast the deciding vote, the church community

is better served when an environment is created that permits struc-
tured and disciplined open-information sharing. This means that focus groups, study groups, or task forces are formed to guide the work
of different individuals to reach a conclusion that can be proposed to
the larger community for acceptance. In essence, they are building a
process to reach consensus—they can agree to disagree—instead of
creating a win-or-lose environment.

THE CHURCH COMMUNITY IS BETTER SERVED WHEN AN ENVIRONMENT IS CREATED THAT PERMITS STRUCTURED AND DISCIPLINED OPEN-INFORMATION SHARING.

Bishop Marcus Matthews is the resident bishop of the Upper
New York Episcopal Area and the president of the General Board of
Higher Education and Ministry with The United Methodist Church.
He has served in a variety of roles in his nearly forty years in ministry,
which has given him valuable insights on how to help congregations
work toward reaching consensus. Bishop Matthews told me about
these experiences and insights.

In my first Church Council meeting, there were those who
were extremely well versed in the *Book of Discipline*. Rather
than being open to embracing a new way of conducting the
meeting, they were entrenched in following a process that
continued to create that win-or-lose mentality. The harder
I tried to introduce a let's-discuss-and-agree approach, the
more they pushed back with *Robert's Rules of Order*, "Is there
a motion on the floor?" In my mind, I knew we needed each
other in order to move things forward. In their minds, it was

still a matter of giving up power, position, and control, rather than reaching consensus. One of the things I knew to be true was that we needed to shift from "win or lose" to "we agree to disagree."

What was more important than establishing a position was developing a strategy to maintain a position of leadership that would empower the congregation to have the same vision I had. We needed each other, and we needed to support and hold each other accountable for making sure everyone had an opportunity to be a part of the decision-making process. Moreover, as stated earlier, there were those who were extremely well versed with regard to the *Book of Discipline* and the authority the pastor did and did not have. I did not want the *Book of Discipline* to be the primary focus when it came to guiding our decision-making process. My preference was for us to allow the Word of God to guide us in how we were to relate to one another. Mark 12:31 says we are to love our neighbor as ourselves, and no other commandment is greater than that. My thought was that we would understand that, even if we did not like each other, we were called to love one another, and through this love we would be able to accomplish a whole lot more. This did not mean there would not be disagreements. However, they would not be as venomous and vile as they had been in the past. We would also understand that we needed to talk to each other and not at each other.

Losing to Win

One of the first things I do in a large-group meeting is establish guidelines and parameters for communicating. However, instead of just listing them, I ask the participants what the rules should be for this meeting. They will begin to name items like "show respect," "don't interrupt," and "don't make it personal," to name a few. It won't be long after the meeting has started that they begin to break their own rules. The good news is that because they have named the rules, I can always interject when the meeting gets out of hand, "You said these were the rules." This allows me to stay in control of the meeting without it seeming as though I am trying to control them.

Another important element of establishing the opportunity for us to talk to one another and not at one another is that I solicit a volunteer to write the rules down for us. This technique again allows me to be in control of the meeting without being in control of them. Periodically, I will ask the individual who wrote the rules down to remind us of the rules. This is the beginning of establishing the process of laying the foundation of accountability. Prior to this, many of the meetings were conducted in a manner that was not representative of individuals being adults, much less Christians. Shouting matches ensued, tempers flared, and nothing was accomplished.

NO LONGER DOES THE PASTOR HAVE TO REESTABLISH ORDER ALONE; THE COMMUNITY AS A WHOLE DOES IT.

By providing an opportunity for the congregation to hold each other accountable, the one who violates the rules understands that he or she is in the minority. In other words, no longer does the pastor have to reestablish order alone; the community as a whole does it, thus eliminating the unfortunate occurrence where the pastor has to engage in a one-on-one with a belligerent member. The most common mistake a leader makes is allowing himself or herself to become emotionally attached to the situation at hand and losing sight of available tactics that can be used to diffuse a volatile situation. More plainly put, the leader should first focus on level-setting emotions and maintaining focus on the core issue rather than on demonstrating to the community at large that he or she is in control. Sometimes you have to be silent. Sometimes you have to allow it to appear as though you are losing in order for you to win. The objective is to reeducate, train, and retrain so that mutual accountability is the order of the day.

SOMETIMES YOU HAVE TO BE SILENT. SOMETIMES YOU HAVE TO ALLOW IT TO APPEAR AS THOUGH YOU ARE LOSING IN ORDER FOR YOU TO WIN. THE OBJECTIVE IS TO REEDUCATE, TRAIN, AND RETRAIN SO THAT MUTUAL ACCOUNTABILITY IS THE ORDER OF THE DAY.

Nearly all families have experienced a situation that caused a big blowout. Angry outbursts happened, cross words were exchanged, and individuals departed the scene in a huff, vowing to never speak to one another again. An event that was originally intended to be a time of family fun turned into a colossal mess. Thankfully, one person always became the self-appointed mediator who hung in there and tried to get the opposing parties to at least sit down and talk to one another. Regardless of whether it took days, months, or years, there was always one who vowed that the family would stay together. In some cases, the feud would continue until there was a tragedy, and then people would soften up and think about coming together. It is always at the funeral that people are able to recognize that life is too short to be at odds with someone over such trivial matters. The same sentiment should exist in the church. It should not be at the closing of a church due to dwindling membership numbers and an inability to financially sustain operations that members decide to come together. We need each other in order to move the vision forward and ensure that the congregation is vital and the ministry is relevant.

My good friend Bishop Walker, mentioned in chapter two, learned this sentiment early on and told me about it:

> I've discovered while pastoring the Mount Zion Baptist Church of Nashville, Tennessee, that we are better together. Where there is no vision the people perish, but where there are no people the vision has no chance. The success of our ministry has been primarily due to congregational buy-in and support. Early on I would hear people ask, "When are y'all going to do this or that?" I knew then that there was a problem of engagement, and if the vision was going to come to fruition, people had to see their role in the manifestation of it. When Paul speaks of the body in 1 Corinthians 12, he indicates that every part of the body is significant, regardless of its function. Often those smaller parts have greater impact on the body's functions. Nobody thinks about their ankle until it gets hit. Once hit, the entire body limps. Everybody can't be the head or arms or legs. Some folks have to be the ankle working behind the scenes. These are the folks who are vitally important to the fulfillment of the vision. Whether your name is called or not, you must find your place in ministry and serve at maximum capacity. Everyone is important, and every role is vital. You are necessary!

In dealing with any issue, it is imperative that the pastor emphasize to the members that they need each other to get the job done. You can do this by using a method I've adopted in the past: preaching a coordinated sermon series and offering Bible studies on the plight of the children of Israel and their wandering in the wilderness. At one of my appointments I preceded my children of Israel series with a sermon series on the vision and mission statements of the church. By focusing on the vision and mission statements first, I was able to point to several reasons why the Israelites had to endure as much as they did. My basic talking points included their lack of faith in the promises of God, their unwillingness to support the leadership, and their continual focus on their personal possessions instead of on God's providential provisions. Those two sermon series and Bible studies helped spiritually ground us so we could move forward with the business side of expanding the ministry. We needed to know how to embrace each other with all of our differences and celebrate each other's gifts and abilities all along the journey. After all, we are all a part of God's body.

CHAPTER SEVEN

I'M IN A DIFFERENT PLACE

No Longer a Member, Now the Leader: When Promotion Comes from Within

When I was a student in the fifth grade, there would be times when the teacher would have to leave the room. Before leaving, she would select a student to be in charge while she was out. Being in charge meant that you would be responsible for making sure the other students did not get out of line while she was away. The student would get to sit at the teacher's desk and keep a watchful eye on the class. If anyone misbehaved, the designee was to write that person's name on the board and report the infraction when the teacher returned. I would always volunteer to be the one to be in charge of my classmates. I perceived this to be an honor and took pride in doing a good job. It never occurred to me there was a reason no one else would volunteer for this dubious distinction. After all, I was in charge; the other students had to listen to me, and if they did not listen or if they misbehaved in any way, there would be consequences! As the class monitor, I possessed the power to make someone's life miserable. I finally realized no one wanted this responsibility because it meant you would be breaking ranks with your friends and having to rat them out, or tell on them, and ultimately get them in trouble. Despite the fact that being the class monitor was a promotion and looked good on your report card, accepting the job caused you to be in a different place. If you told on the unruly students—many of whom lived in your neighborhood, rode the same bus as you did, played with you at recess, and sat with you at lunch—you put yourself in a different place from them.

Promoting from Within

One of the most common situations many have to deal with is when promotions are granted from within the organization. The change or blessing must be dealt with by those receiving the promotion and by those whose friends are promoted. This is a concern because in most, if not all, of the cases there is a shift in the relationship. The new expectations and level of responsibility necessitate a different protocol for effectively carrying out one's new assignment. This is an extremely common occurrence within The United Methodist Church. Local pastors are often identified to be promoted to the level of district superintendent. The district superintendent position is responsible for overseeing several other churches in different geographical locations, known as districts, within a larger geographical area, called an annual conference. The natural process of such a progression dictates that selections are made from within the ranks. The promotion itself is not the issue, but rather *how* the promotion is handled when it comes to maintaining relationships with others who have not been selected for the promotion. If not handled properly, then the behavior of those who are not promoted most often changes in a negative manner, and it becomes challenging to serve as a manager.

Before promotions are given, relationships between the leader and person interested in the promotion have already been formed. Because relationships have usually existed for quite some time before a promotion is given, decisions need to be made as to how the relationships will be handled in the future. Some of the questions that should be considered include: Do you continue to come together socially, and if so, to what degree? What are the expectations concerning sensitive information being shared? How are discipline issues going to be handled? The old saying "It's just business" does not speak to the emotional toll that mishandling promotions from within can take. Careful consideration must be given when selecting leaders from within the existing community. One of the more prevalent considerations is whether the individual selected is able to maintain a commitment to choose to do the right thing rather than choosing sides.

Making the Shift

When members of the congregation are selected to become leaders, there must be a shift in behavior and relationships in order for them to be effective leaders. The leader needs to implement an extremely thorough training program in order to begin to reshape cultures and highlight expectations. Almost immediately the new leaders must recognize that they have been called to a different level of service. They must learn how to serve the people but not get caught up in all of the stuff that goes on with the people. For instance, there are some individuals who feel as though they should be involved in everything that goes on in the church and every decision that is made. If they are not directly involved, then they become the ones who try to thwart or sabotage any efforts or initiatives put forward. Additionally, they may solicit the help of the leader who has been selected from among the congregation. Depending upon the leader's level of spiritual maturity, it would be no problem for the disgruntled member to pull the leader and others out of their roles of supporting the vision of the ministry.

NEW LEADERS MUST REC-OGNIZE THAT THEY HAVE BEEN CALLED TO A DIFFER-ENT LEVEL OF SERVICE. THEY MUST LEARN HOW TO SERVE THE PEOPLE BUT NOT GET CAUGHT UP IN ALL

OF THE STUFF THAT GOES ON WITH THE PEOPLE.

Selecting leaders from the congregation is a challenge for the new pastor because, in most cases, he or she will not have had ample time to vet the membership to comfortably identify the best candidates and places of service for them. In The United Methodist Church, for instance, pastoral leadership changes are made in June of each year. When a new pastor arrives, he or she inherits what is already in place. This includes, but of course is not limited to, mind-sets and behaviors, facilities, structure, order, and financial condition. Also, depending upon the predecessor's length of service and work ethic, either a culture of excellence or a culture of "we couldn't care less" might exist. The best-case scenario is when the opportunity is presented for the formation of structure and order as if it was nonexistent before.

In a United Methodist church, leadership selection and development is the responsibility of a nominations and leadership development committee. As the chair of this committee, the pastor is called to guide the work of the team to select the best leadership from a wide cross section of the congregation. This is one of the committees wherein the members serve in classes of three years. The challenge is when the pastor is new and the team members on the committee have been in place for some length of time and formed relationships with the membership. Another challenge is the fact that the incoming pastor has to manage the team he or she inherits. Depending upon the existing culture, this can be positive or negative. If the group has decided it wants to keep the new pastor under its control, it can influence the voting and the behavior of the chairs of the other committees. When this is the case, the new pastor must focus on creating a critical mass of new members and riding out the tenure of those existing members who are unwilling to lead in a manner that reflects Jesus' teaching of "love your neighbor as yourself" (Mark

70

12:31 NRSV). Waiting for their tenure to expire will be painful and frustrating; however, it allows time for God to transform hearts, and it will give the new pastor time to focus on building relationships with incoming members instead of trying to gain control of an uncontrollable situation.

WAITING FOR THEIR TENURE TO EXPIRE WILL BE PAINFUL AND FRUSTRATING; HOWEVER, IT ALLOWS TIME FOR GOD TO TRANSFORM HEARTS, AND IT WILL GIVE THE NEW PASTOR TIME TO FOCUS ON BUILDING RELATIONSHIPS WITH INCOMING MEMBERS INSTEAD OF TRYING TO GAIN CONTROL OF AN UNCONTROLLABLE SITUATION.

At one point I was focusing on gaining control of people instead of implementing a sound training program to develop leaders and begin to shape thinking. I chalk it up to immaturity and desiring to establish myself as the leader, or the one with the power. My behavior and mind-set caused me to be the one making a contentious situation even more contentious and leaving the "spectators" questioning my leadership ability, rather than questioning the behavior of the "saint" who was causing the commotion. I had to learn that a training program would be the pivotal piece in changing expectations and establishing a new culture, not trying to change established behaviors. Another mistake I made was leaving people in positions of leadership for too long. The leaders were doing a great job, the people were responding, and we were getting things done. Everyone was happy, and I did not have to work as hard. Not rotating the leadership as prescribed by the *Book of Discipline* caused me more pain and work in the end than if I had followed procedure. The first lesson I learned as a new leader was that, while it may look and feel good on the surface, things may not be that healthy on the inside. The second lesson I learned was that the saying "Familiarity breeds contempt" is more than just an age-old adage. Someone coined it for a reason!

Discerning Friendship from Faithfulness

Careful attention must be given to fully understanding why people call you friend or want to be your friend. John 15:13 reminds us, "There is no greater love than to lay down one's life for one's friends" (NLT). We can all agree that few relationships like the one described in this scripture passage exist. Being in a different place as a leader means navigating the road between friendship and faithfulness to the call and cause of Christ. There are those who will infringe upon the friendship in order to ask for favors of you as a leader that could place you in a compromising situation. They know what they are asking for is wrong, and they know you have committed yourself to a different level of service. The moral dilemma arises from being caught between doing the right thing and sacrificing your ethics for the sake of saving a friendship. I once encountered a situation that involved a leader sharing information that had been discussed in a meeting, even after everyone in the meeting had agreed to keep the conversation confidential. We wanted to wait until further discussion could take place and more facts were uncovered. It was an extremely sensitive personnel matter and should not have left the room. Nevertheless, the member who violated the confidentiality agreement and, more importantly, the covenant agreement to keep it confidential gave into the "friendship" pressure.

After this breach of the confidentiality agreement, I had to decide whether to address the situation with the individual or address it ministry wide. I decided to address it from a system-wide perspective. I chose not to do so right away, however, because I did not want to seem retaliatory in my action, thus creating instant rejection of any idea I put forth to deal with future breaches. I concluded that what was more important than correcting one individual was correcting a system that supported behavior that was inconsistent with the type of leadership team I was trying to create. Being in a different place meant much more than physical locale or place of service; it meant that a different level of spiritual maturity needed to be displayed. With this in mind, I focused on developing a leadership training program that would encourage individuals to begin to rely more heavily on their spirituality.

During the next leadership training session, I decided to ask each leader to sign a covenant agreement and a confidentiality agreement. The covenant agreement focused on the spiritual nature of the connection with the other team members and established the premise that participation on a particular committee was more than just taking care of business. It meant being about God's business. More plainly put, the team members' actions and behavior should serve to edify, or build, the body of Christ and not destroy it. It was clearly stated in the agreement that a violation would result in immediate dismissal from the team with no committee action required. There were those who wanted to challenge me on this decision, as the *Book of Discipline* makes no mention of a covenant agreement or a confidentiality agreement. But, in a pastoral and nonthreatening manner, I responded that while the *Book of Discipline* does not address the issue, the Bible does, and I would rather be bound by the directives of God than by a set of rules and regulations that, while extremely helpful, do very little for spiritual formation. Furthermore, our first priority should be to lead in a manner that shows the congregation that more important than getting the business handled is the fact that the leadership team is a Christ-centered and spiritually mature group of individuals who are passionate about doing God's work. In order for this to be accomplished, the leadership team needs to be engaged in spiritual formation opportunities, collectively and individually. To be in a different place means that movement must occur. Too much focus is given to physical movement or activity when in essence the spiritual movement, or spiritual growth, is the key driver that ensures solid and sound leadership development. As in the corporate sector, a sound training program ensures that employees are equipped to get the job done effectively and with maximum productivity. Just as there are periodic training courses and refreshers, the same should be the case in the church. It is unfortunate that the mind-set of some is that of being just a volunteer and of feeling that mediocrity is acceptable.

OUR FIRST PRIORITY SHOULD BE TO LEAD IN A MANNER THAT SHOWS THE CONGREGATION THAT MORE IMPORTANT THAN GETTING THE BUSINESS HANDLED IS THE FACT THAT THE LEADERSHIP TEAM IS A CHRIST-CENTERED AND SPIRITUALLY MATURE GROUP OF INDIVIDUALS WHO ARE PASSIONATE ABOUT DOING GOD'S WORK.

Church or Corporation?

All too often individuals will vehemently state that the church needs to be run like a church and not like a corporation. My contention is that there is nothing wrong with the corporate model as long as the spirit of the people using the corporate model is right. The corporate model, which is extremely helpful in outlining roles and responsibilities, keeps the operation running smoothly. I like to use Chick-fil-A as an example. While other establishments are open practically twenty-four hours a day, seven days a week, Chick-fil-A is closed on Sundays and yet leads the fast-food industry. All Chick-fil-A employees are encouraged to visit their house of worship. They are not told where to go, just to go. Additionally, when you visit the Chick-fil-A headquarters, you immediately encounter their mission, vision, and core values statements. There is order and clarity of purpose in the air. That is to say, when you walk through the doors, you immediately understand what this company is about. It would be fair to say that you are put in a different place. The same should happen in our churches, in that everything that we do—the way that we lead and the service we provide—should put the people who walk through our doors in a different place.

THE WAY THAT WE LEAD AND THE SERVICE WE PROVIDE SHOULD PUT THE PEOPLE WHO WALK THROUGH OUR DOORS IN A DIFFERENT PLACE.

CHAPTER EIGHT

SPIES IN THE CAMP

Dealing with Individuals Who Seek to Destroy
the Vision

I mentioned earlier that I am an Army brat. My dad was in the Army for twenty-seven years and did two tours of duty in Vietnam. The type of warfare they were engaged in was classified as guerilla warfare. The basic premise was that there were no rules for the enemy. The American troops had a set of rules to play by called rules of engagement, but the other side did not. Instead, they would disguise themselves by wearing the uniform of the friendly troops and embed themselves in the camp. There would be no way to tell the friendlies from the enemies. At an opportune time, the enemy would inflict serious and deadly harm. All too often innocent civilians would suffer as well. They would be going about their daily tasks, not suspecting that they were about to be caught up in the fray. Many blameless individuals were killed simply because there were others who were not concerned about the people injured or killed.

How to Identify the Spy

Many times when a leadership transition occurs, the logical expectation is that changes will occur. These changes will require near-perfect execution in order to be effective and accomplish the goals and objectives set forth by the leader. However, before getting to the point of executing the plan, the right team must be in place. This team should consist of a trusted few who will carry out the mission to the masses. I am intentional about saying "a trusted few" because those who carry the message must do so in a positive manner and in a way that will incite and excite individuals to at least give change a chance. In most organizations there are those whose mission in life is just to create chaos and stir up confusion. Even though the change is necessary, certain individuals will simply refuse to assist in making it happen. I do not understand why they do what they do; I just know that they do it.

Before getting to the point of executing the plan, the right team must be in place.

Shortly after I arrived at one of my appointments, a longtime member suggested I bring together a group of people who could help me get my vision out and serve as advocates for me as their new leader. Being new, I was ill prepared to enlist the support of anyone. After hearing his suggestion, in all honesty, I was not ready for this to take place, nor was I comfortable with meeting with any particular group. I knew that this could set me up to be in a position to alienate a group of individuals who could cause me tremendous heartburn later on. I was also unsure about whether this member's motives were pure. Unfamiliar territory can become a testing ground for those looking to identify or capitalize on any weak points, a fertile ground for foolishness. A new leader must have discernment when entering into this type of situation and be realistic about the fact that everyone who wants to work with you may not want to see you succeed. I told him I would pray about it and get back to him.

Unfamiliar territory can become a test-

ING GROUND FOR THOSE LOOKING TO IDENTIFY OR CAPITALIZE ON ANY WEAK POINTS, A FERTILE GROUND FOR FOOLISHNESS.

As we all know, when we say, "Let me pray about it," we are using code language for, "I really do not want to do this, so give me some time to figure out how to get out of it!" After I had considered various ways to handle the situation, I decided that the best course of action was to figure out how I could minimize my presence and place this member in a position of ownership over the entire concept and process. So I suggested he help me by calling together a group of individuals he thought could be trusted, and I asked if he would serve as the lead facilitator for the group. This would allow for him to expose himself if he indeed was the enemy.

I knew that, regardless of the tactics I employed, if any problems arose, it would be his word against mine by the mere fact of his being a longtime member who was respected by the entire congregation. But this was not a major concern in that I knew that the less I said the better off I would be. In other words, I let him know that I thought his idea was great, put him in a position to move it forward, and made him feel as though the success of this leadership transition was totally dependent upon what he had put into motion. Some would say that this classifies as a form of manipulation, but I would contend that, to a large degree, his support and his voice were extremely vital to the success of the leadership transition. While he could be designated as a spy in the camp, I saw an opportunity to use his possible passion for destruction as a weapon for my defense.

I am sure he thought I would openly and readily jump at the opportunity to put together my own group and garner support from individuals I did not even know. Admittedly, on the surface his was

79

a great idea; it would have been extremely helpful, and I could have leveraged my exposure to my handpicked group to hopefully gain some allies. But there was a nagging feeling that kept me asking myself, "What is his motive for suggesting this?"

Destroyers of the Vision

I'm sharing this experience because I think being extremely transparent is necessary. It may appear as though I'm in a state of constant paranoia about the motivations of church members. I will also admit I often have conversations with myself about situations. (However, as the joke goes, "I'm sure not to answer myself.") I'm not at all paranoid; I just think it's important for new leaders to use the experience I have just related to more fully process opportunities that are presented and to refrain from being too eager to accept any and all proposals that on the exterior appear to be extremely vital to success. I had to learn to take my time to evaluate situations before committing to them because when I was a new pastor, I found myself to be the worst spy in the camp. Basically, I could have been destroying my own vision. I could have been classified as a double agent. I was giving information to both sides of the camp. I was so eager to get the job done and so trusting of everyone that I responded very openly to various questions without first processing the question or the response and going one step further to determine how the recipient would use the information.

For instance, one individual stopped me after a Sunday worship service and asked me what my vision was for the church as we embarked upon a building project. I was so excited to have an opportunity to share my vision that I immediately rattled off what I was imagining. In rapid-fire succession I began to spout out everything I believed we should have. "I see a multipurpose facility with the worship space that doubles as a gym, more classroom space, a computer lab, and a common area that's also a food court." With great exuberance I described how the youth would be responsible for managing the food court, including its marketing, sales, and inventory. In the middle of a sentence it hit me, "He isn't interested in your vision. He wants to get information to take back to the group that is against the expansion." You see, up until this point, I had been silent about my position. I had vehemently stated that it was extremely important for all of us to arrive at a place of consensus based on what we felt God was requiring of this ministry.

Because I had already played my hand and revealed my position, because I had just been a spy in the camp, I needed to figure out how the information I had shared would or could be used against me. It did not take long for the person to whom I had revealed my vision to attempt to use what I had said to cause the membership to reject the notion of even considering expanding. He began to inform the membership of how I planned to get them deep into debt with my big dreams. He went on to state that I was trying to build a new building so that I could make a name for myself. The most damaging statement he made was that my motives were not pure and that my intentions did not have the best interest of the church at heart. There was no way I could stop the harm this would cause, so I had to figure out how to once again come from behind. The only thing I could think of was the fact that, even though I was the leader, I needed the support, or more specifically, the vote, of the congregation before anything could be done. Moreover, the direction we were taking had to be based on the demonstrated and verbally expressed needs of the congregation. I had also previously said that it would take all voices to adequately determine the needs of the congregation and that my position was one of facilitating the conversations in a manner that would let the ministry move forward to serve the community.

My focus was to not respond in a panicked, reactionary way but to utilize the information to my benefit by being truthful about what I had said and keeping the congregation focused on the process that every United Methodist church must adhere to in a building program. This process ensures that no single individual possesses the power to make a unilateral decision concerning the property and indebtedness of the congregation. Trying to tactfully discredit the spy, myself, and refocus the membership was difficult, to say the least, but the goal was accomplished. The key was to not let the situation become emotionally charged. I had to remain focused and get the people back on course. After all, my excited and hasty response put us in this position in the first place.

You can be your own worst enemy.

Maintaining Calm during Chaos

When dealing with individuals who have committed themselves to destroying the mission and the vision, it is important to understand that you can be your own worst enemy. It is imperative to resist becoming emotionally vested to the degree that your only thought is getting back at or getting rid of the individual causing the disruption. Emotions cause us to lose clarity and engage in behavior that is more destructive than that of the spy. While easier said than done, the leader must maintain his or her composure and always choose a course of less destruction. It means being cool, calm, and collected, when in actuality you would love nothing more than to blow your top. I can recall being yelled at and called a liar to my face in front of a small committee meeting. I allowed the encounter to continue until there was a point at which I could interject. Then I invited the individual to provide proof to substantiate his claim. Of course, there was no evidence, and the only thing he could say was that he had been told about what I had said. In front of everyone, I invited him to bring the person or people who had provided him with his information so that we could all meet, and I also invited the group we were currently in front of to join us. He declined, and the group concluded that he really did not have anything to base his accusations on. I can honestly say that my blood was boiling while I was standing there being yelled at and called a liar. But maintaining my composure yielded me a tremendous amount of social capital that I would definitely need to cash in on at a later date. While most individuals would have placed a *W* in the win column and progressed on to the next game, I knew that now I needed to move quickly to keep this member on the team, just in a different place. The worst thing that could happen would be to leave him alone to think of some other destructive way to thwart the efforts to move forward.

THE LEADER MUST MAINTAIN HIS OR HER COMPOSURE AND ALWAYS CHOOSE A COURSE OF LESS DESTRUCTION. IT MEANS BEING COOL, CALM, AND COLLECTED.

Before we all left the room, I reached out to him and said I was glad we had gotten that behind us so that now we could move on to do what God had called us to do. I initiated conversation about our having to reconcile in front of everyone, since the altercation had taken place in front of everyone. I must pause here and make sure you understand that this was not what I was feeling in my heart, but I knew it was something that needed to be done, and perhaps I would feel it in my heart later. At that moment, however, I needed to demonstrate exceptional leadership ability and not jeopardize the future of the ministry. Fortunately for me, he responded positively, albeit in a gruff and cavalier manner, and we were able to end the night in a better place than it had begun. After the two of us had had our conversation, I went around the room, pointing at the members and asking them one at a time if they would like to share anything that would help us move forward in a more Christ-like manner. No one said anything, so I went one step further and asked that this incident not be shared outside of the room. Now, you know just as well as I know, that someone was going to get on the phone and it would be all over the congregation before morning. Nevertheless, I made my request to demonstrate another facet of mature leadership.

Spies in the camp can be managed in such a manner that their behavior can be channeled in a positive and constructive way rather than a negative and destructive way. It all hinges upon the leader's ability to always stay focused and not let ego or emotion get in the way. It means spending a tremendous amount of time nurturing and cultivating relationships with individuals who will act as Jonathans. We can read the story of David and Jonathan in 1 Samuel 19. King Saul became jealous of David and devised plans to kill him; however, Saul's son, Jonathan, helped David escape the traps. The Bible says there was an immediate bond of love between David and Jonathan, and they became the best of friends. They let nothing come between them, not even career or family problems, and they drew closer together when their friendship was tested. In essence, their relationship had a commitment to God first and a commitment to each other second. What's even more compelling is that the relationship was formed before Saul became angry with David. Yet even after Saul expressed his dislike for David, the relationship between David and Jonathan continued to grow and become stronger. The most common occurrence in a church is that once one person falls out with another in the life of the church, individuals start choosing camps and the battle begins. What we can learn from this biblical narrative is that the most important aspect of dealing with spies in the camp is to make sure that solid teaching is done with regard to being in relationship with God and not a denomination, a building, or any particular group.

LEADERS MUST SPEND A
TREMENDOUS AMOUNT OF
TIME NURTURING AND CUL-
TIVATING RELATIONSHIPS
WITH INDIVIDUALS WHO WILL
ACT AS JONATHANS.

CHAPTER NINE

CELEBRATING SMALL VICTORIES

Appreciating Everyone's Accomplishments and Affirming Others' Contributions

I used to be one of those people who had the toughest time understanding that the best way to eat an elephant is one bite at a time. My mind-set was such that anything less than everything was nothing. In other words, it was always all or nothing. Win at all costs because losing was not an option. Well, as life continued to chip away at me in the form of one defeat after another and one overwhelming situation after another, I realized I needed to hurry up and grasp the concept that small victories are just as important. You do not have to accomplish it all in one day. You do not have to have a colossal success every day, and you do not have to view every situation as win or lose. Although it may appear on the outside as if all is lost, I discovered there are instances when, even in the midst of a potentially losing situation, a winning situation is being set up. One of the many things I learned was how to not lose the war by fighting a battle that is not worth fighting. In other words, I could not allow myself to become emotionally engaged in destructive conversations, mutinous movements, turf wars, or anything else that would keep me from celebrating the small victory already won. Now, I must insert here that I was not oblivious to and I did not ignore the rebellious and riotous behavior of a few individuals. Nevertheless, I knew that if I was going to survive as a leader, I would need to learn how to celebrate small victories even in the face of conflicts more intense than Armageddon itself.

Course Correction

There are many opportunities for leaders to find themselves in a position where they are constantly acknowledging the same people over and over again or only acknowledging those individuals whose contributions directly impact the congregation in a way that is significant to the leader. There are also times when some individuals want to be recognized for every little thing they do. If you are not calling their name, then they are salty or disgruntled and begin vowing to not do anything else for you or the church as long as you are there. It is extremely important to always be cognizant of recognizing everyone's contributions so that some do not feel as though they are not an integral part of the ministry. Celebrating small victories is more about a collective celebration than issuing individual accolades and acknowledgments.

CELEBRATING SMALL VICTORIES IS MORE ABOUT A COLLECTIVE CELEBRATION THAN ISSUING INDIVIDUAL ACCOLADES AND ACKNOWLEDGMENTS.

When attempting to change the course of an organization that is already in motion, and has been in motion for quite some time, you must understand that the change will not occur quickly. When a cruise ship's captain gives the order to change the course of the ship, it takes some time before the ship actually makes a change of direction. Someone has to enter the coordinates into the computer and then the computer has to read the data it has received. After all the necessary components have been engaged, the ship begins to respond ever so slowly. The turn is gradual and methodical so as not to disturb the passengers onboard. Anything too abrupt could disrupt a calm and relaxing time for someone. Unless you are standing on the deck and taking notice of the external indicators like the wake, or waves, behind the ship or the orientation of the ship's bow, or front, you do not feel the effects of the change. The only indicator for you is arriving at your port of call, your destination, safely.

Such is the case when changing the direction of an established ministry. Small, incremental steps of change need to be taken. These steps need to be intentional enough that individuals recognize that change is being made but subtle enough that they do not perceive the change as a threat to their existence. The point here is that the objective all along is for the church, like the cruise ship, to arrive safely at its destination. Negotiating the turn without incident is a victory worth celebrating.

Hidden Hazards

Executing a change in direction with a cruise ship may not seem like a big deal. There should be no problem with the turn because there is nothing but wide-open ocean. It is obvious that the ship needs to turn slowly enough so as not to disturb its passengers. But it is not the obvious that trips us up. A computer glitch or an engine malfunction could disrupt the entire process, leaving the ship adrift or floating without power. National attention has been given to mishaps experienced by several cruise ships belonging to a worldwide cruise line company. The ships eventually made it back to port safely, with the training of the crew keeping the situation from becoming even more challenging than it already was. The point here is that changes or turns will be met with unforeseen obstacles. The key is to handle them in such a manner that, despite the negative experience and unpleasant conversations, there will still be a few who remain committed to overcoming the challenges and moving forward.

THE KEY IS TO HANDLE OBSTACLES IN SUCH A MANNER THAT THERE WILL STILL BE A FEW WHO REMAIN COMMITTED TO OVERCOMING THE CHALLENGES AND MOVING FORWARD.

Dr. Emmanuel Cleaver III, senior pastor of the twenty-six-thousand-member St. James United Methodist Church in Kansas City, Missouri, told me that for a new leader who is planning to execute a change in course, the focus must be on the family.

> I think it is critical, when implementing change, that the change agent be seen as a member of the family not a stranger. Too often, pastors go in to a church and begin changing things instantly. The problem with this is it can cause longtime members to feel as though the pastor doesn't care about their tradition and culture. It makes the pastor seem like an outsider coming in to tell us what we ought to do. However, if a pastor takes the time to get to know the people, their likes, history, and values, it lets the people know that the pastor is one of them. It says that we are all in this thing together. That's when you can begin the process of leading change.

> I can remember taking the opportunity at one of my appointments to restructure the worship services so that one of them had a more contemporary approach. I do not have to tell you that when you begin to mess with the worship service you wake up some sleeping giants. The current worship style was not attracting new worshipers, and, quite frankly, those who were attending were doing so only out of loyalty because they were not excited about it but merely tolerating it.

The proposed change was based on the fact that the worship service served as the main point of entry for membership in this church. If we could get more people interested enough to just stop by for a visit, we could possibly increase the number of new members. I met with the Worship Committee and Church Council chair, and I asked a member of the Staff Pastor Parish Relations Committee to attend as well. Prior to this meeting, I had discussed the idea with the Worship Committee chair, the Church Council chair, and the Staff/Pastor-Parish Relations Committee member individually. The intent here was to begin the process of trying to turn the ship. I wanted to make the request and then have the individuals who would have to buy into the new course of direction give me feedback up front as to what could potentially happen to keep this from being a time of celebration. When this small group gathered for our meeting, I first thanked them for their support of the transition the church was going through. I told them that it was because of them and their love for God, and for their church and the generation coming behind them, that this ministry would continue to be as successful as it had been in the past. I thanked them for allowing me the opportunity to partner with them to lead such an awesome church.

This could be classified as schmoozing, but I like to think of it as letting the existing community know that I understood that I could not approach them in an arrogant and uncaring manner with my only concern being to accomplish an objective to make myself look good. This thought would be on the minds of some anyway, but it did not keep me from laying the groundwork for us to celebrate a victory.

As the Ship Turns

The small group had great questions. Some of the questions had obvious answers, but I had to remind myself that it is not the obvious that trips me up. The question that tripped me up was about the type of music that would be played at the restructured worship service: Would we still sing the hymns? The three questions I then quickly asked myself were: Who asked the question? Who is that person connected to in the congregation? What might the group be looking for in my answer? The first thing out of my mouth was, "What a great question!" Then I went on to explain that it would be a blended service with blended music. What this meant was that we would sing all types of Christian music. If this did not work, I reassured them, we could always come back together to take a look at other options that might fit a little better. The person who had asked the question seemed okay with my response. I had already asked the Worship Committee's chair to schedule a full committee meeting to begin immediately following this small group meeting. Scheduling a full meeting in this manner was risky but necessary. It was risky in that if the small group had not agreed with my proposal, I would have been in a fix. However, I had a default plan in place. If there had been disagreement with my proposal for the restructured worship service, I would have asked everyone in the small group to identify for me what they thought needed to happen in order for us to increase the attendance and ultimately the membership. I would have taken their thoughts and presented them to the full Worship Committee as things we would work on and come back to discuss at a later date. Scheduling the two meetings back-to-back was necessary because I could not allow time for the contents of the small group meeting's discussion to get out in a manner that would have set me up for defeat even before I had had an opportunity to present a plan.

The full committee approved the plans, and we moved forward with a more contemporary style of worship, retaining some of the core elements, such as the Lord's Prayer and the Psalter reading. We eliminated giving visitors the microphone to tell us where they were from and who they were visiting. We created an actual worship service for the children and called it Children's Church. The children were checked in by parents and their service was held at the same time as the normal worship service; it ended at the same time as well. Many churches have a "Children's Moment" where the kids come down to the front of the church and hear a short biblical story from the pastor or ministry leader. This was a significant change for our church. We also added more praise and worship time. The service was not showy or performance laden. It was not chaotic, but Christ centered. Basically, we just livened it up and encouraged people to move from spectating to participating. Thanks to God the changes yielded great results. On one Sunday, approximately thirty-six people joined the church. They indicated that they had been visiting for some time and decided to go ahead and join because they liked the direction the church was moving in. To add to the success of this change, the people who joined were young families with children.

After approximately three months of a steady increase in attendance at the restructured worship service, I called the full Worship Committee back together, as well as the chairs of the Church Council, Staff Pastor Parish Relations Committee, and, of course, the Worship Committee. I thanked them all for their support and praised them for the results. One committee member said, "Pastor, it wasn't us who did this. It was you and your preaching! The people who joined were responding to your preaching." I immediately replied that such was not the case. As a team we all had a part to play in how God had increased our numbers. We all had to be open to and embrace change. We had to make sure we had the right spirit about why we were doing what we were doing, and we had to understand that if we continued to work together, God would favor our ministry and continue to bless our work. Everyone was important to the ministry moving forward. No one person's contribution was greater than any other's. Quite honestly, I was surprised I did not get more pushback from individuals thinking that I was going to eliminate the traditional service in favor of a more contemporary one. On the contrary, we needed both worship service styles so that we could continue to expand our reach. After this experience, I could see our ship was beginning to turn ever so slowly so as to not upset those who were on board, but at the same time, it was making enough movement to let people know that this ministry was going somewhere and now was the time to get on board and join in the celebration.

93

The Mindset of the Leader

It is extremely difficult to leave your ego at the door, isn't it? Especially if you are accustomed to constant victories and very few, if any, setbacks. Victories and successes, especially piled on one after the other, can facilitate a false sense of self-awareness. It is imperative that, as a leader, you do not allow yourself to be lulled into a mind-set of invincibility and total self-reliance. In order for the ministry to be positioned for change, the leader must have already made a change spiritually, mentally, and emotionally. A spiritual change means that the leader makes a deeper commitment to studying and meditating on God's word. A mental change empowers the leader to stay focused on that which will benefit the entire community and not to personalize every situation that arises. Emotional change strengthens you as the leader, so that you do not allow your emotions to control you and you do not try to take on everyone who disagrees with you or challenges your ability to lead.

One of the most important things to note is that in positioning the ministry to change direction, I had to stay focused on celebrating the victories even if that meant celebrating what had been done before I became the new leader. It is extremely easy to allow insecurity and ego to cause you as a new leader to try to erase or minimize all that occurred with the previous administration. No matter how aggravating or agitating it may be, it would behoove you to affirm members as they recount what has been done. Listening to the history will let you know how engaged the person telling the story was. The history will also help you understand the sentimental value that is attached to certain ministries or traditions of the church. There is a balance that must be struck, because you do not want to foster a culture of nostalgic living or paralyze future progress by holding on to the famous seven last words of a ministry: "We've never done it that way before!"

The mistake is made when there is an aggressive effort to establish yourself as the new leader and to create instant victories. The tragedy

94

here is that the impression that is made is one wherein you are only concerned with making a name for yourself and thus have no regard for the welfare of the existing community. Once this perception is cast, it is extremely difficult, if not impossible, to dispel it. It is for this reason that you must overcommunicate your vision in a conversational manner. The conversation will give the membership the opportunity to feel a part of the vision and in most cases sign on to at least give it some thought. I do not mean to make it appear as though all you have to do is talk to the people and they will instantly love the idea. There will always be those individuals who will not agree to anything that represents change and takes them out of their position of authority. The natural inclination is to work around them or ignore them. I have found that an attempt to work with them and include them in the future direction of the ministry will benefit you in the long run. Prayerfully they will be influenced to at least give the new direction a chance.

The apostle Paul speaks of an effective leader being one of influence, helping people to change their thinking and ultimately, their behavior. Paul uses his ministry to the church at Thessalonica to speak to how leaders should care for the people. In I Thessalonians 2:7-8, Paul tells Timothy, "Though we might have made demands as apostles of Christ . . . we were gentle among you, like a nurse tenderly caring for her own children" (NRSV). It is here that Paul also illustrates how effective leadership depends on how well the leader is able to balance getting the job done with developing a caring relationship with the people.

Five Ways to Celebrate the Victories

Too often when the word *celebration* is used, the connotation associated with it involves something that comes with great fanfare and expense. However, such is not the case. Here's a list of five ways victories can be celebrated. These are just a few basic suggestions to get you thinking about how to recognize and celebrate the "wins" at your church:

1. Does your church publish a newsletter, either in print or online? Include a photo and brief write up of the individual or individuals and their accomplishment. Perhaps this is something you could do in each issue.

2. Recognize the honoree during the worship services or other all-church gatherings. Make a pulpit announcement, inviting the honoree to stand, and then invite the congregation to show their appreciation with applause. Perhaps you might lead the congregation in a prayer of gratitude for this individual.

3. If the victory had an impact on the community, invite an elected official to join the congregation on a Sunday morning. The official can offer thanks to the congregation and mention how vital they are to the betterment of the community.

4. Connect with your local or neighborhood paper, and ask them to publish an article or feature discussing the victory and naming the individuals responsible for it.

5. Invite the individual or group of individuals to position themselves at the front of the room or at the exits when the service concludes so that the congregation can shake their hands and even extend a hug of appreciation.

These are a few ways you and your congregation can intentionally show appreciation for a job well done!

CHAPTER TEN

WE'VE COME THIS FAR BY FAITH

Maintaining Focus on God's Will and God's Word

At the writing of this book, my first, I have had to take a reflective look at my life. There have been so many times when I have found myself in situations that seemed as though they would cause me to say the heck with all of this church stuff. I do not feel like dealing with these people anymore. When I would reach the point of what I thought was no return, there would be the strongest urge inside me to get over it and keep pushing. After all, I had not come as far as I had based on my own abilities and resources. It had to be God who had kept me in this race this far, this long.

During my last year at Hampton University (formerly Hampton Institute), I found myself in a situation where I was not sure if I was going to graduate. I had been so successful at everything and now was facing the ultimate embarrassing moment of not graduating. I had pledged Kappa Alpha Psi fraternity and run for, and won, the office of senior class president. I was a student leader and received the senior superlative of "most likely to succeed." But now I was not even sure I would be leaving with a diploma in my hand because I was out of money and out of time. To make matters even more challenging, my father had been diagnosed with lung cancer and given until April of 1985 to live. My graduation was scheduled for May of that same year. I had to graduate. I had to get out so I could get a job and take care of my mother. This was the conversation going on in my head, and my thought process was of wishing I could be in a place where I could embrace walking by faith and not by sight (2 Cor. 5:7).

It was through this experience of multiple uncertainties that I learned just how God is able to take control when I "let go and let God." I had to learn to be concerned with and not worried about, focused but not fretful. I had to learn, as the apostle Paul put it in Philippians 4:11, how to be content in whatever state I found myself. I did not realize at the time that I was being prepared to allow my faith in God to take me to places that my imagination could fathom and where my intellect would not be able to sustain me. The faith factor would be an integral part of my journey and my ability to handle opportunities, whether positive or negative, as they came my way. I define the "faith factor" as the willingness to believe and act on the fact that God is able to work it all out no matter what it is: "And we know that all things work together for good to those who love God, to those who are called according to *His* purpose" (Rom. 8:28 NKJV). The faith factor is sometimes working against popular opinion and scientific data to accomplish that which is seemingly impossible. The faith factor allows you to understand that such workings are neither by your power nor your might but by God's Spirit. Faith causes you to get out of bed and go into the next day with passion and purpose, despite having suffered a monumental defeat or setback the day before.

Which Way Do I Go?

As a leader you will experience days that will literally take almost all the life out of you. As the late Bishop Cornelius Henderson thought, everyone will have a Good Friday, but hold on because Easter Sunday is coming! Allow your faith to keep you on the journey. The journey starts with an individual's level of faith. A leader's personal level of faith and personal life of devotion and prayer, as well as personal worship and praise, bleed into what he or she has been called to do when leading an organization or a congregation. It starts within and serves as a sustaining factor of more consequence than all of the leadership development training opportunities in the world. The most important aspects of a leader's life are practicing sound spiritual discipline and maintaining focus on God's will. I can without hesitation say that the mistakes I have made and the bad judgment calls I have acted upon have all been because I detoured from sound spiritual discipline and began to act upon my will and not the will of God. You may say that doing God's will is good common sense. I would respond that good sense is not so common when you are in the throes of life.

THE MOST IMPORTANT ASPECTS OF A LEADER'S LIFE ARE PRACTICING SOUND SPIRITUAL DISCIPLINE AND MAINTAINING FOCUS ON GOD'S WILL.

I was appointed to my first church with the instructions to go and cut my teeth and get some experience. It was a small-membership church, and the North Georgia Conference had not expressed any real plans for the church. When this opportunity was presented to me, I was living a great life as an associate pastor. All I had to do was what I was asked to do by my senior pastor. I lived in the parsonage because he and his wife owned their own home. The people loved me, and I loved them. I was able to preach frequently and truly enjoyed the ministry. Now I had the opportunity to be the one who was in charge. Before I go any further, I must say what everyone already knows: the journey is much different when you are the one in the driver's seat. You do not have time to take in the sights along the way. You do not have the luxury of making too many wrong turns or going down a dead-end road. You have to at least have a reasonable idea of where you are going.

At the time of this appointment, MapQuest was still being perfected, the car I drove did not have a GPS in it, and I was not that good at reading a map. Basically, I would be feeling my way around to get to the destination. This assignment would prove to be my "walking by faith and not by sight" experience, starting with actually getting to it in the first place.

When I arrived, I was excited and nervous all at the same time. This was my first appointment, and I had to succeed. All I had was the experience my senior pastor and previous church had afforded me and a few good sermons (or at least people had told me the sermons were good). The people at my new appointment were passionate, and the church was located in a growing area. I was eager to get in place and start things moving. I had it all planned. In fact, I had drawn up personalized thirty-, sixty-, and ninety-day plans. I was ready to schedule meetings with each family in the church and primed to kick off my first Sunday service. We were ready to rock 'n roll! However, the message that kept coming to me as I prayed and prepared for my new role and responsibility was that, more important than having a few good sermons, I demonstrate having sound spiritual discipline and a passionate desire to do the will of God. The beginning of the journey with this congregation had to be one founded on faith in God and submitting to God's will. They needed to see me demonstrate sound spiritual discipline in my prayer life, study life, and worship.

Part of my thirty-day plan included guiding the church in planning for growth, both spiritually and numerically. Before we even began the conversation about growth or future plans, I decided to do a short-term Wednesday night Bible study on the spiritual authority of God's word. My thoughts were simple and straightforward. Either we were going to take God at God's word or not. Either we were going to be led by the Holy Spirit through prayer or not. The study took eight weeks and included a workbook to help individuals process the material that was discussed in the Wednesday night service. The level of excitement and participation in the study was phenomenal. I anticipated individuals attending the first night just to see what was going on and then deciding they did not want to participate for the full term. However, we had almost 100 percent participation. The lesson content focused on how Jesus continued to state that he had come to do the will of his father who was in heaven. The intent was to motivate the congregation to continuously engage in prayer and focus on God's will for the ministry. We needed to be conscious of the fact that the journey was going to be a faith journey.

Run the Race with Patience

It has often been said that the church is full of runners. Some are sprinters, and some are marathon runners. The key is to figure out who is who and then get them into the race. The participants of the Wednesday night Bible study served as my core group for beginning a discussion around what they thought God's will for the church's ministry was. This discussion became the basis for the Wednesday night service. I formulated questions related to discerning God's will and incorporated scripture to demonstrate how different individuals in the Bible prospered when they followed God's direction. I also used passages of scripture that illustrated how there would be challenges even when God has given instructions. The challenges did not have to destroy the community but could be used to strengthen it as it continued to focus on God's will and God's word. Each of us needed to do what we had been gifted to do and make sure that all along the journey we were making a contribution.

Despite all of the scripture and prayer and teaching and preaching, there were those individuals who did not want to embrace the fact that we were gearing up for growth and that things would not be as they used to be. No longer would everyone know everyone, and no longer would it be the close-knit community that it used to be. They would have to get used to the fact that we needed to make room for those whom God would send to us. To them this represented giving up their territory and sharing their space. I knew I could not battle these individuals, so I enlisted the help of those who did embrace the new direction. I started using the Wednesday night service to point out that God had anointed and appointed us to accomplish the Great Commission. Matthew 28:18-20 reads:

> Jesus came and told his disciples, "I have been given all authority in heaven and on earth. Therefore, go and make disciples of all the nations, baptizing them in the name of the Father and the Son and the Holy Spirit. Teach these new disciples to obey all the commands I have given you. And be sure of this: I am with you always, even to the end of the age." (NLT)

The journey we were on was not about anything other than bringing others to Christ and demonstrating the love and grace of Jesus. In order to do this, we had to go out and get them and invite them into our sanctuary. We needed to have ourselves together and our house in order before we invited anyone in. We needed to make sure we as individuals had adopted spiritual disciplines, both personally and corporately, that caused us to always be sensitive to God's will and not our own. We needed to be sure we had enough of God's word in us that when we shared the story of Jesus we were doing it from our hearts and not our heads. That is to say, we had to be able to articulate our journey before Christ and how the journey had been after Christ. We needed to be able to tell newcomers that it had not been easy for us but that it had been made bearable because we were not on the journey by ourselves. With each passing day, each of us was being prepared to lead someone else to a better way.

The transformation did not take place overnight, and then there was the constant need for reminding the congregation of what we were supposed to be doing and why we were doing it. There were frequent instances of individuals getting off track and out of focus with what God had called us to do. There were small factions of members who would pop up from time to time with proposed ministry opportunities that did not fit the scope of the vision or mission of the church. To manage these instances, I made sure that small group studies continued around the vision and mission. This ensured that everyone would at least be aware of the fact that we were on a journey and the course had already been set by God's word. All we had to do was devote ourselves to doing what God had called us to do and stay focused on that task with each passing day.

Because there were more who signed up to do God's will, the ministry continued to grow spiritually and numerically, and we were able to purchase fifteen acres of land and build a new church. The testimony here is that the church did not have the financial resources to purchase land in the area, nor did the church have the financial history that would make it an attractive candidate to any lending institution. Nevertheless, because of the church's faith and passion for God's word and God's will, a lending institution said yes! We purchased and built the church. What is more, the ministry continues to thrive to this day. The more important point is that each day needed to start with our personal devotion, and then we could come together, bringing what God had placed in our hearts while we were apart. This coming together and sharing of all things in common demonstrated that God could do anything but fail.

When I think about my senior year in college. I remember the fear and trepidation that consumed my every waking hour. I was paralyzed and nowhere near able to walk by faith and not by sight. Everything I saw was equating to failure. I did not and could not embrace the notion that God was working it out and I simply had to stick it out. What enabled me to get it together and keep pushing was the prayer of a classmate. As I was walking to my dorm room, a classmate saw me and the look of worry on my face. She asked what was wrong and I shared with her my feelings about my fear, my finances, and my father's failing health. She took my hands, and she prayed for me right there in the middle of the sidewalk. People were walking by, and I could hear them get quiet as they passed us. Pretty soon I was focused on her prayer. When she finished the prayer, she told me that I had to believe that God had not blessed me and brought me this far to stop now. In that moment I decided to stick it out and to finish the job and graduate.

103

I witnessed my earthly father sticking it out while God, our heavenly Father, worked it out. He was battling lung cancer and had undergone radical radiation and chemotherapy treatments. He died in February of 1986 after having been able to attend my graduation the previous May. He sat through the long and arduous ceremony, even though he was sicker than anyone could have imagined simply by looking at him. The chemotherapy and radiation had taken their toll on him, but he was there. What occurred to me only as I wrote this particular chapter is that my father dug deep to be there. The doctors told him he would not make it, and the way he was feeling was telling him he would not make it. Yet, he made it. He knew God was working it out, and he just needed to stick it out. He ran his race with patience, and he fought the good fight of faith.

APPENDIX

Reflective Questions

Chapter 1: Hi, My Name Is

1. How often do I find myself bragging about myself or talking about what I have done?

2. During a conversation, am I able to resist the temptation to follow up someone else's accomplishments with my own?

3. Would most people describe me more in terms of my relationship with Christ or my relentless recounting of my accomplishments?

Chapter 2: From Moses to Joshua

1. What are some specific ways I could help bridge the generational gap?

2. Am I intentional about time spent with the Senior Saints?

3. How often are the Senior Saints celebrated for their contributions to the ministry?

Chapter 3: Excuse Me, Where's the Bathroom?

1. Do I provide congregants with the opportunity to share the history of the church?

2. Do I ask questions and stay engaged while the answer is being given?

3. What individual or group do I need to spend time with in order to hear from them and share with them my desire to learn from them?

Chapter 4: Are We Related?

1. Who can help me with the familial connectedness in the congregation?

2. What leaders are related to one another?

3. What affinity groups, that is, military, hobbies, and so on, exist that I can begin to form a relationship with?

Chapter 5: Are We There Yet?

1. Are there any Project Managers in the congregation who can give leadership to the establishment of goals and objectives?

2. Will the project be too labor intensive and become frustrating?

3. Is Christ the focus or is simply completing the project the focus?

Chapter 6: I Need You, You Need Me

1. Is there an intentional effort to make sure as many as possible are included in the visioning effort?

2. Am I giving time to different ministry groups to encourage participation and ensure that their concerns are being heard?

3. What layperson can serve as the "glue" that holds it all together?

Chapter 7: I'm in a Different Place

1. Who has demonstrated that they are a good follower?

2. What congregation-wide messages will serve to set the environment about the expectations of leaders?

3. How often do ministry meetings include biblical examples of individuals transitioning from membership in the clan, tribe, or family to a position of leadership?

Chapter 8: Spies in the Camp

1. Who can help me identify the person or persons who do not agree with the vision?

2. How can I approach those persons to express a genuine concern to hear them? What layperson can assist me with this?

3. Have I exhausted all means to reach common ground? What steps have I taken?

Chapter 9: Celebrating Small Victories

1. Who can be asked to give leadership to the recognition and celebration of the victories?

2. Are the celebrations inclusive of ages, genders, skill sets, educational levels, economic levels, and so on?

3. What are we doing to make sure the same person or group is not celebrated too frequently?

Chapter 10: We've Come This Far by Faith

1. Is there an Intercessory Prayer Group? How often do I meet with them?

2. Do we celebrate God twice as much as we celebrate the people?

3. What am I doing to hold on to my faith in God no matter how challenging my current position may be?

About the Author

Reverend Dr. Marvin Anthony Moss

The Spirit of the LORD is upon Me,

Because He has anointed Me

To preach the gospel to the poor;

He has sent Me to heal the brokenhearted,

To proclaim liberty to the captives

And recovery of sight to the blind,

To *set at liberty those who are oppressed;*

To proclaim the acceptable year of the LORD.

—Luke 4:18-19 (NKJV)

The Rev. Dr. Marvin Anthony Moss is the senior pastor of Atlanta's historic Cascade United Methodist Church. Since his arrival to Cascade in June 2006, more than 1,300 members have joined the church and more than fifty ministries perform outreach services to the local, national, and global communities. Prior to serving at Cascade, Dr. Moss served as senior pastor at St. James United Methodist Church in Alpharetta, Georgia (1999-2006). Under his leadership there, St. James grew from fewer than 200 members to more than 1,200. Additionally, the congregation purchased fifteen acres of land, and a new edifice was erected. Prior to serving at St. James, he was associate pastor at Wesley Chapel United Methodist Church in Decatur, Georgia.

A frequent guest of President Barack Obama's National African American Clergy Leaders Group, Dr. Moss shares concerns for human equality and civic and civil rights with lawmakers, leaders, and congregants. He has testified on Capitol Hill before a Senate Hearing Committee on the long-term effects on the unemployed. He is the founder of the newly formed Cascade Community Development Corporation, which will provide an incubator for new and small businesses, revitalize depressed areas, and provide economic empowerment opportunities in the Cascade Community. Cascade's outreach programs have been featured for their ability to serve "the least of these." The ministry reaches thousands of Atlanta area residents through numerous programs, including its clothes closet, which features free clothing and household items; men's shelter feedings; recidivism programs; and a yearly "Thanksgiving Basket" program, which provides Atlanta area residents with a week's worth of groceries during the Thanksgiving season. In 2011 Cascade presented Morris Brown College President Stanley Pritchett with the monetary donation that helped the struggling college settle its debt to the U.S. Department of Education.

Dr. Moss and Cascade have been featured on CNN, BBC, TBN, The History Channel, NPR, and The Atlanta Journal Constitution. His weekly syndicated radio devotional minute, "Living Through the Not Yet," has been a favorite of Radio One listeners, while his "Streaming Faith" devotionals garnered followers worldwide.

Dr. Moss is a native of Goldsboro, North Carolina. He is a graduate of Hampton University and the Naval Chaplains Reserve Officers School, and he holds a Master of Divinity degree from Gammon Theological Seminary at the Interdenominational Theological Center (ITC) and a Doctor of Ministry degree from Drew University. His extensive childhood travel, a result of being "an Army brat," gave him a unique insight into different cultures and a passion for people of various ethnicities and experiences.

Dr. Moss is a member of Kappa Alpha Psi fraternity, 100 Black Men of Atlanta, and Leadership Atlanta Class of 2011. He is involved in the greater Atlanta community at many levels. He is on the Gammon Theological Seminary Board of Trustees; he is a member of Gulfside Association, Inc. Board of Directors, a member of the Cristo Rey School of Atlanta Board of Directors, and a member of the Board of Directors with The Foundation for Public Broadcasting in Georgia. He was the recipient of the Denman Evangelism Award for Church Growth in 2011 and 2003 and the NAACP Emancipation Award, and he was inducted into the Morehouse College Martin Luther King Jr. Board of Preachers. He received the Gammon Theological Seminary 2011 Distinguished Alumnus Award. He is also the recipient of the Whitney M. Young, Jr. Service Award from the Boy Scouts of America.

Dr. Moss continues to preach with purpose, lead by example, and focus on his ultimate mission: Kingdom building. He is excited to share his first book, *Next: Surviving a Leadership Transition*, and is looking forward to writing more publications in which he can share practical principles, Christian council, and faith-based options for enhancing the viability of and increasing the sustainability of any organization.

CPSIA information can be obtained at www.ICGtesting.com
Printed in the USA
LVOW06s2313291013

359151LV00002B/2/P